THE CHOWCHILLA

The Ethnohistory of a Yokuts Tribe

Second Edition, Revised and Expanded

Robert Fletcher Manlove

B O O K S

Fresno, California

The Chowchilla: The Ethnohistory of a Yokuts Tribe
Second Edition
Copyright © 2020 by the Chowchilla Tribe, Jerry Brown, Tribal Chairman.
All rights reserved.

A previous edition of this book was published under the title
The Ethnohistory of the Chowchilla Yokuts

Cover illustration: Detail from *Indians in Council, California* by
Albert Bierstadt. Circa 1870; oil on canvas. With permission from the
Smithsonian American Art Museum, Washington, D.C.

Published by Craven Street Books
An imprint of Linden Publishing
2006 South Mary Street, Fresno, California 93721
(559) 233-6633 / (800) 345-4447
CravenStreetBooks.com

Craven Street Books and Colophon are trademarks of
Linden Publishing, Inc.

ISBN 978-1-61035-366-3

135798642

Printed in the United States of America
on acid-free paper.

Library of Congress Cataloging-in-Publication Data on file.

For the Chowchilla Tribe, past and future.

Contents

Acknowledgments

This work could not have been done without the active assistance of the Chowchilla leaders: the tribal chairman, Jerry Brown, and members of the tribal council, Abigail Franco, Bart Topping, and Roger Venturi. These leaders of the tribe initiated the project by visiting my home and asking me to assist them in collecting historical materials that could be used in an application for federal recognition. They provided funds from a Chukchansi grant in support of the first eight months of the research in 2010, reviewed and approved my report, and elected to publish it under the title *The Ethnohistory of the Chowchilla Yokuts* in 2012. During the subsequent eight years, I continued collecting data pertaining to the Chowchilla ethnohistory while producing a similar report for the Tsi Akim, a Maidu Nisenan tribe. During that period, Tribal Chairman Brown was particularly helpful in guiding my searches and going out to other tribal members to find the answers.

By 2018, I decided that I had sufficient material to publish the upgraded and expanded second edition of the book you are now holding. I am particularly indebted to Chairman Brown during the completion of the second edition for his guidance and clarification of crucial issues. I also want to express my appreciation for the assistance of the librarians and staff at the University of California in Berkeley in acquiring additional books and documents and thus accelerating my research. I also have a debt of gratitude for my wife, Ruth, for editing and suggesting parts of the manuscript that could benefit from further clarification. Lastly, I want to express my gratitude to my publisher, Kent Sorsky , and his talented assistant, Jaguar Bennett, at Linden Publishing, for their very much appreciated support and patience needed in the final steps of publication.

Transfer of Royalties
and Copyright Notice

I contend that a tribe's history belongs to the people of the tribe and only to the people of the tribe. It is, thus, immoral for an author to profit from the sale of the history. For this reason, all royalties received in the sale of this book are to be given to the Chowchilla Tribe. The leaders of the tribe have told me that their primary goals for the future are (1) federal recognition, (2) the improvement of the health, education, and general living conditions of the native people in the area of their homeland, and (3) to do this without building a casino. I heartily support these goals and I hope that the funds from the publication of this book will assist them in achieving them.

The copyright of the book is also transferred to the tribe when it is published. No copies or changes of the book, in full or in part, can be made without the permission of the author before it is published or without the permission of the tribal council after it is published. The author takes responsibility for any misinterpretations or errors in the published book but not for errors or misinterpretations that are added after publication, with or without the approval of the tribal council.

Prologue

Several years ago, the leaders of the Chowchilla Tribe came to my home to ask me to collect all of the information about their tribe available and write a summary of their history that could be included in an application for federal recognition. This would be a difficult task because most of the information about their tribe was buried in sources that were written for entirely different purposes and buried further in very large collections, such as, for example, the federal records in San Bruno, CA, and the massive collections in the libraries of the University of California.

Federal recognition is absolutely mandatory for the survival of a tribe in the context of American culture and they were very anxious to submit an application, if possible, within a year. Consequently, I agreed to help them as much as I could, even though I was working with another tribe, the Tsi Akim of the Nisenan Maidu, at the same time. I started collecting information about the Chowchilla as time allowed and, about eight months later, I delivered a preliminary report to the Chowchilla leaders for the purpose of supporting their federal recognition application. The tribal council was very pleased with the report despite the fact that only with more research would it be complete. They say that it would help with their application because it was the first document published that focused exclusively on their tribe and it contained information about the tribe that they had not seen before. For these reasons, they quickly reached a consensus to accept the report as it was and to have it published for distribution among the tribe's membership. I was uneasy about the decision because I regarded the report as a work in progress. Nevertheless, the report was a description of their tribe and, as such, it was the property of the tribe upon acceptance. The tribe could reproduce the report in any manner that they wished.

In the years since then, I have continued accumulating information about the Chowchilla tribe, impelled by the desire to help them by presenting a more complete version of their story, but also by the desire to reveal the terrible destruction of the Chowchilla homeland that has happened over the last 170 years. Their territory was partly in the flatlands of the San Joaquin Valley and partly in the undulating foothills of the Sierra Nevada Mountains. Being attracted to and the salmon they held, the tribe's people gathered in villages along four major waterways, the San Joaquin River, the Fresno River, the Chowchilla River, and Bear Creek. They lived in semipermanent villages with adjunct fishing places nearby to gather the salmon as they came up the rivers twice a year in unbelievable numbers. The people of each village also made annual pilgrimages to the majestic black oak forests at higher elevations where they gathered acorns and hauled tons of them back to store in village silos and to use for months thereafter.

When settlers arrived in the 1850s, the beauty of the Chowchilla land astonished them. Some were overcome and wept for joy. Beautiful meadows lay before them decorated by handsome evergreen California live oaks scattered across the landscape and by water-loving cottonwood and sycamore trees along the rivers. The meadows were thick with wild oats and bunch grass. Wildflowers displaying great splashes of vibrant colors elevated the meadows into a form of natural art. Astonishing clouds of multicolored butterflies flew among grazing herds of elk, deer, and antelopes. Overhead, the skies were periodically darkened by huge flocks of duck, geese, and other migrating fowl.

In contrast to this abundance and beauty, the Chowchilla land today is shockingly destroyed. The wild oats, the wildflowers, and the clouds of butterflies are all gone. A foreign type of grass has replaced the native bunch grasses. There are no salmon to be fished now; the rivers are meager, intermittent streams reduced to dry beds most of the year. The hilly area is dry and nearly uninhabitable. Big swampy areas have developed in the flatlands that might provide fishing opportunities except that the marshes are rimmed with thick growths of impenetrable tule and produce clouds of thirsty mosquitoes. Some lakes out in the center of the valley are also impossible to fish because they are nearly completely covered by tule. The migrating fowl no longer come through in great waves. The great black oak forests in the hills have been decimated, first by hogs eating all of the acorns and later by American settlers taking all of the timber that they wanted.

How did all of these things happen? The answer to that question is a story within the Chowchilla story, because the forces that changed the environment were the forces that changed the Chowchilla. In the following pages, both stories must be told.

It's the past that tells us who we are.
Without it, we lose our identity.

—Stephen Hawking

1

The Chowchilla and Their Homeland

Before the Spanish, Mexicans, and Americans came, there were 40 tribes living in the great San Joaquin River Valley of California. They were scattered over the 15,000 square miles in the Valley but they all spoke the same language, called Yokuts,[1] with local variations (dialects). Like other Yokuts tribes (who are now better known), the Chowchilla were peaceful hunters and gatherers who had lived in harmony with their environment for many thousand years. When the invaders came, however, they emerged as a tribe that would not step aside to avoid them. Instead, the Chowchilla saw that the invaders were voracious thieves who took and destroyed the land, rapaciously killed the animals and plants, and enslaved the native people. With alliances with other Yokuts tribes, they became warriors who were known throughout the native people of California.

It is thus shocking that, despite this great honorable bravery, the Chowchilla are little known to the people that now walk their land and, for this reason, the book in your hands is dedicated to compile and set down their tumultuous history, to honor their lifestyle and their struggles to maintain their freedom and sovereignty. First, we will concentrate on the tribe before the invasions, establishing the location of their land and the number of people. Then, in the next chapter, we will explore the nature of their traditional culture.

Where was their homeland? From reports of Chowchilla conflicts with the invaders and the locations of neighboring Yokuts tribes, we know that they lived in what is now called the Madera, Merced, and Mariposa coun-

---

1. The name *Yokuts* is both singular and plural, appearing as *Yokutch* in transcriptions of Yokuts languages.

ties of California. Further, we know that Yokuts tribes logically used rivers as their boundaries. As mentioned above, this stemmed from the dependence upon the salmon. Every tribe needed the salmon and, for peace and cooperation, adjacent tribes drew their boundaries at the middles of the rivers. Adding to this observation, we know (1) the location of Chowchilla village sites, (2) the location of neighboring tribes, and (3) the places at which American settlers collided with Chowchillas, and all this information suggests the Chowchilla boundary to the southeast as the Fresno River, the southwest boundary as the San Joaquin River, and the northwest boundary as Bear Creek, as shown on the map on page 3.

All of these boundaries are approximate, of course, but we can solidify them with the following data. The San Joaquin River is supported as the southwest boundary primarily by the identification of Nupchenchi villages *opposite* the mouths of the Chowchilla River and the Mariposa Creek.[2] And there were battles between native warriors from the north side of the river and Spaniards camped at Nupchenchi villages on the south side. In one significant battle, warriors from the north, probably Chowchilla, trapped and repelled a well-armed troop of Spaniards.[3]

On the southeast side, the Fresno River is well established by incidents at the boundary and the villages of neighboring tribes. There was an argument at that river between the Chowchilla and the Dumna about the boundary, for example.[4] Farther up the river, the tribe on the other side of the river was Chukchansi, and it is well known that they held Coarsegold Creek, a tributary of the Fresno River flowing southwest. In fact, Gayton has established that Chukchansi villages continue toward the southwest until they are only six miles from the river at Hensley Lake.[5] The Chowchilla/Chukchansi boundary, however, was a decidedly porous one, allowing easy access of each tribe to the land of the other tribe. There is a long history of Chowchilla/Chukchansi friendship, cooperation, intermarriage, and the sharing of resources, and this warm relationship continues today.[6] The Chukchansi, for example, had constant access to basket-making materials located in Chowchilla territory.[7]

---

2. Wallace 1978:470.
3. Phillips 1993:57–58. This battle is described in chapter 3.
4. Kroeber 1925:481–486; Gayton 1948:153.
5. See Gayton 1948; Kroeber 1925:523.
6. This is demonstrated by being allies in the Mariposa War (chapter 6) and by cooperation concerning a modern rancheria casino described in chapter 12.
7. Gayton 1948:176.

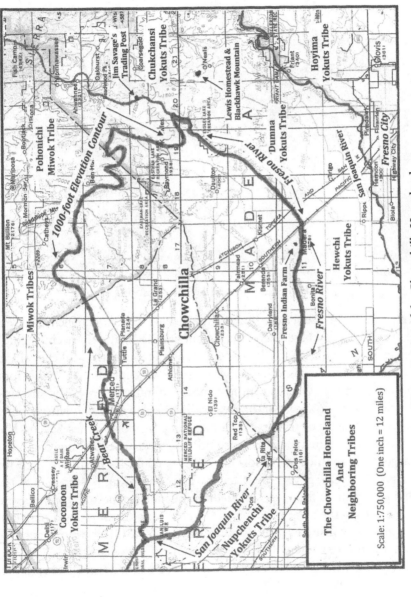

Figure 1. Map of the Chowchilla Homeland

3

Figure 2. Chowchilla River in spring

There is one incident near the boundary with the Chukchansi, however, that needs to be discussed here. In December of 1850, the Chowchilla chief, Jose Rey, and his warriors held an important meeting with Chukchansi and other Yokuts and Miwok chiefs and warriors to discuss what was to be done about gold-crazed American miners pouring into the area. The meeting was held at a shallow part of the river called Fresno Crossing where James Savage, an American trader, had built a trading post. James Savage had indirectly caused the violence by providing a place where whites could use their gold to buy food and tools and natives could also bring in gold for trade goods. A U.S. government agent, Adam Johnston, was present at the meeting, hoping to find ways of quelling the violence between miners and natives. During the meeting, many chiefs rose to speak, but most important was a speech by Jose Rey directly addressing Johnston as the representative of American government: "This is our country," Jose Rey stated. "Why do the Americans come here? They are good and brave but they come upon

Figure 3. Berenda Slough marshland near Chowchilla River, swollen with spring runoff. *Courtesy Bowman Looney.*

the land of my people. What do they intend to do? I want to know, and I must know, *right now!*"[8]

His words might be interpreted as identifying the land at the Trading Post as Chowchilla land and, indeed, when he did not receive an acceptable answer from Johnston, he ordered his Chowchilla warriors to attack and destroy the trading post a few days later, killing any Americans hired by Savage to run the Trading Post. However, there are multiple reasons why Jose Rey might *not* have meant that the Post was on Chowchilla land. First, his words were probably in the Yokuts language and translated by James Savage who had lived with Yokuts people. Savage may have added an American point of view with the first-person possessive pronoun, *my,* instead of *our.* Also, American historians, who diligently searched for the location of Savage's trading post as a place for his grave, concluded that it was four miles from Coarsegold in Chukchansi territory, as shown on the map and, most important, Chowchilla today do not claim that land as

8. Letter from subagent Adam Johnston to Commissioner of Indian Affairs, L. Lea, in Washington dated March 7, 1851 (italics in Johnston's report to the American government).

Figure 4. Foothill area near a village site

Chowchilla land. Thus, the words of Jose Rey were most likely referring to the land of all of the tribes meeting to consider war against the American miners and not the land of any particular tribe.

With regard to the northeast boundary of the Chowchilla homeland, the boundary was determined by the elevation that the Chowchilla were likely to go to collect acorns and to establish permanent occupation. They lacked clothing and other personal protection against the colder temperatures,[9] so it is likely that they went to higher elevations only in the warm fall days when acorns were falling. At that time, the main concern was to gather as many acorns to last the villages below for at least a year. For that reason, they generally went up to the elevation at which large oaks grew and produced the acorns that they preferred. The oaks they sought were, consequently, the Black Oak or Blue Oak that grew at about 1,000 feet elevation and dropped large masts of acorns. At the chosen location, each family had a traditional location at which they built a shelter for the time they stayed there.

---

9. They had rabbit skin robes but these were very difficult and time-consuming to make and were consequently owned only by men and women of great age and distinction.

The homeland boundary in this area can logically be established at 1,000 feet elevation and, with the considerable variation of the 1,000-foot contour, the boundary line shown on a map should be very wiggly. The map on page 3, consequently, shows a rough average of the location of the 1,000-foot contour.

Now that we have the boundaries on the map, we can calculate approximately the area of the homeland and, with this, we can get an approximation of the population of the Chowchilla. The area of the homeland was measured in two ways. One method was to determine how many small areas of graph paper can be put into the map area. The unit used in this method was arbitrarily a rectangle measuring 0.53 square miles; 1,850 of these fit within the map area of the homeland. The second method employed a very sensitive device to determine the weight of the paper inside the map boundaries (0.65 ounces) and comparing it with the weight of the paper within the boundaries of the whole rectangular map (2.10 ounces). The first method gave 1,010 square miles as the area of the homeland and the second method gave 987 square miles, so we may say the homeland area was approximately 1,000 square miles.

Now, using the area of the homeland, we can get an estimate of the Chowchilla population. This is done by calculating the average population density for the Yokuts as a whole and using that number with the tribe's area. Alfred Kroeber is the source of the total number of Yokuts people, which he gives as 18,000 people from the mouth of the San Joaquin to Tehachapi Mountains.[10] Combining that number with the size of the Valley, 15,000 square miles, we have the best estimate of the population density, 1.2 people per square mile. Using the size of the Chowchilla homeland, we come to the conclusion that there were approximately 1,200 Chowchilla before AD 1800.

Now, with basic knowledge of the location and size of their homeland and the size of the tribe at the beginning, we turn to the nature of their lives in that time frame in the next chapter and then we may concentrate on the book's main objective, namely, to describe the effects of many external forces that changed the Chowchilla to what it is today.

---

10. Kroeber 1925:486, 883. Neither Kroeber nor any of informants he uses to write his 1925 book actually lived with and studied Yokuts tribes. However, none of the anthropologists that have worked among the Yokuts since then have seriously challenged his estimate of the total number of people that lived in the San Joaquin Valley before the beginning of the nineteenth century.

2

Chowchilla Culture
Before Contact

The underlying goal of this ethnohistory is to describe and explain the changes forced upon the Chowchilla by foreign invaders. However, when one wishes to describe such change, one must know the circumstances of the tribe before the changes. For the Chowchilla, this is a big problem; records describing their culture before contact with the foreigners do not exist. Further, it is very likely that the Chowchilla culture went through important changes during the early years of interference and there are no records explaining what those changes were from the native people's point of view. Consequently, there are many question marks in the basis of change that occurred later. The best we can do is to reconstruct the precontact culture from carefully chosen historical sources and use that as the starting point for studying change.

There are three types of historical data that might possibly be useful in doing this. First, there are descriptions of the precontact culture that have been passed down from generation to generation to current day Chowchilla people. These descriptions are important because they provide information about early events from the native point of view. However, such information tends to be episodic and incomplete. It is also difficult to determine the social context in which a change occurred. For example, why did Jose Rey, the paramount chief of the Chowchilla who was incarcerated in a mission for several years, come back with a Spanish name without changing it back to his natal name? There are multiple cultural attributes that might have influenced that situation. A second source of information might be the diaries of nonnatives who were temporarily in contact with the Chowchilla soon after contact. There are very few of these[1] and, as would be expected, they have a nonnative perspective.

The third and most useful source consists of ethnographies written by anthropologists that describe the precontact cultures of other nearby Yokuts tribes. The ethnographic information of twelve Yokuts tribes that was gathered by A. H. Gayton is particularly useful. Gayton interviewed descendants of each Yokuts tribe in the 1925–1928 time frame. Three of the twelve tribes—the Chukchansi, Dumna, and Choinumne tribes—were close neighbors of the Chowchilla and can be used to reconstruct a good approximation of the Chowchilla precontact culture. The only problem with using Gayton's data was that she was a perfect ethnographer, gathering information without bias or judgment. When an informant contributed an obviously modern perspective, she adds it without evaluation. In addition, an informant might describe cultural components that reflected more distant societies, rather than the Chowchilla. The Chukchansi, for example, were closely associated with the Miwoks, who spoke a different language and had a distinct culture. Gayton's Chukchansi information may have resembled Miwok culture more closely than the Chowchilla culture. The Dumna culture that Gayton describes as precontact is another example; it showed distinct signs of being influenced by Spanish mission culture. In startling contrast with other Yokuts cultures, she reported that the Dumna believed that God and his Son created the world.[2] As a result of this good reporting, her description of the Choinumne culture is probably our best source of information about the Chowchilla, even though the Choinumne Yokuts were farther from the Chowchilla. Linguist Christopher Harvey supports this conclusion in his study of nine Yokuts dialects.[3] Harvey found that the Chowchilla dialect was structurally closer to the Choinumne dialect than to any of the other seven dialects. The Chowchilla dialect had one more consonant than the Choinumne dialect but all of the other 30 consonants were identical in the two dialects. The other seven dialects had at least four consonants that were different from those of the Chowchilla dialect. This is important because, when any two tribes have very similar languages, it means that there must have had frequent interactions, as in trade relations and intermarriage, and, hence, had developed very similar cultures.

---

1. Eccleston's diary, published in 1957, is an example.
2. Gayton 1948:28.
3. Christopher Harvey, Indigenous Language Institute, University of Manitoba, compared nine Yokuts dialects (cf. www.languagegeek.com/california/yokuts.html).

We can also be certain that the Choinumne culture described by Gayton was their precontact culture because we can compare her description with a description from someone who lived among the Choinumne. In 1850, Thomas Mayfield's family built a cabin across the river from a Choinumne village and became close friends with the native people. Later that same year, Thomas' mother died unexpectedly and his father and older brothers had to seek employment on a ranch. Thomas was then only six years old, too young to be much help on a ranch and, when the Choinumne invited Thomas to stay with them, his father decided that that would be best for him. Thomas consequently spent ten formative years growing up in the manner of Choinumne children. His narration of those years, recorded by Frank Latta in 1920, provides an invaluable account of Choinumne culture and of Chowchilla culture as well. The remainder of this chapter gives a general description of precontact Chowchilla culture that emerges from the considerations above.

All of the adults in a village were busy from an early morning bath in the river to the evening meal around a fire. Some stayed in the village during the day to do the long and tiring work of preparing acorn meal to cook and to make the many indispensable baskets. Others left the village in small groups to hunt and gather. Although some tasks were traditionally performed by one gender or the other, women and men commonly worked together. In the fall, men climbed the oak trees and used poles to shake down the acorns for the women to gather and transport to the silos at their village. In the winter, men and women would be found gathered in a house or ramada (wall-less shade structure) to make baskets of many types. Men hunted deer and antelope while the women were actively butchering and transporting meat to the village. Young people learned hunting skills by hunting smaller animals with scaled-down adult tools and methods. When all had returned in the evening, they exchanged information and analyzed the day's events. Social change was slow after thousands of years living in close harmony with an abundant environment. There was an annual pattern—what they did one year, they would do the next year—but change was what the environment and weather required rather than for social improvement or religious ritual.

The diversity and abundance of food sources were phenomenal in precontact times. Black oaks of the Sierra produced their favorite acorns[4]

---

4. Black oak acorns had more fats than other types of acorns (Heizer and Elsasser [1980:95–96]).

in abundance. The grasslands provided many edible seeds and plants. Large numbers of deer roamed the foothills and amazingly large herds of elk and pronghorn antelope were found on the flatlands. Salmon swarmed the San Joaquin River and its tributaries twice a year with so many fish that the natives could frequently catch and dry enough for the winter in one week. Waterfowl in the sloughs and rivers were abundant. Beyond these resources, there were many types of small game (pigeons, rabbits, squirrels, etc.) and insects (grasshoppers, caterpillars, yellow jackets, etc.).[5] There were occasional times when food was scarce and, when this concerned acorns or salmon, they were very serious. In some years, the black oaks might fail to produce significant numbers of acorns or the salmon run might be sparse, but, by storing acorns in big silos and drying more salmon than was generally needed, these times would pass with temporary shifts in diet. Generally, the Chowchilla and their neighbors in the Sierra foothills did not need to go far to find alternative types of food.

The Chowchilla villages were composed of tepee-like family houses and hemispherical sweathouses. Both of these were 10 to 20 feet across at the base and thatched, not with mats or animal skins as you might find elsewhere, but with willows or long grasses that grew along the edges of streams and lakes. The families could build their houses anywhere they wished and, as a result, villages had no predictable order. Many Chowchilla villages were built along a stream or river, and, in these cases, the chief's house was commonly at the west end of the village. His house was built with the same construction as the other houses, but it was larger in diameter for several reasons. It was a mark of his status, a meeting place, a shelter for visiting chiefs and messengers, or a place for healing. Sweathouses were men's places in which they cleaned themselves each morning with sweat followed by a swim in a stream or lake. Unlike villages in other tribes north of the Yokuts (e.g., the Maidu), there were no large roundhouses where ceremonies were held and where the families could seek shelter in the winter.

Chowchilla families were patrilineal, meaning that a family consisted of all of the men and women that are related through a particular male line (lineage). A family house would typically include a married couple, their children, and other unmarried relatives. The wives of the men in a house were from a different lineage but all of the men, unmarried women, and children were from a male lineage. This means that the Chowchillas did not consider themselves related to their own mothers or anyone in their

---

5. Heizer and Elsasser 1980:103–108.

mother's family line. They would, on the other hand, consider themselves related to all people in the tribe who were even remotely related through their father's lineage. One result of this was that patrilineal cousins of a similar age (father's brother's children, father's father's brother's children's children, etc.) were considered to be brothers and sisters of each other.

It is easy to see that, in this kinship system, there would be many people in the same generation of a family calling each other brothers and sisters. This caused useful cultural features. One of these was a layering of the society into four layers, namely, babies, children, adults, and elders. Children were expected to play at being adults without any responsibility; adults were expected to act individually with loyalty to the patrilineal family; and elders held aloft and advised the family but are not responsible for the family. It was very bad to be impolite to elders.[6] Male children and male elders were discouraged from or not allowed to use the sweathouse.[7] Tribal unity was built on the "brothers" supporting each other; an adult male would sacrifice himself to protect fellow warriors. Women in a "sisters" group acted together to accomplish a chore without being directed to do so and maintained contact with women who married and moved to another house or village. If possible, sisters would marry into the same other lineage, providing a stronger attachment between the lineage of their husbands and their own lineage.

Such loyalty and unity were very important to the Chowchilla, as will be seen in their concepts of kinship and their kin-based social groups. The tribe was composed of about 30 clans, i.e., 30 groups of related families.[8] Each clan was identified by a totem figure (e.g., the eagle clan or the blue jay clan) and each was composed of men and women who would insist that they were part of an extended male line and, hence, related, but who generally lacked any detailed information about how they were related to many of the others. Kinship relations were sufficiently expressed by reference to the totem animal. A person's clan determined the possible social roles that the person could have. This applied to important Chowchilla roles, like tribal chief, tribal subchief, chief's messenger (*winatum*), village chief,

---

6. Mayfield [1929] 1997: chapter 10.
7. Gayton 1948:60, 186, 217.
8. Gayton reported that the Choinumne had 30 clans and that the Dumna had 26. She also reported that her informants from the Chukchansi Tribe remembered only five clans in their tribe, but that no doubt reflects the heavy casualties during the Mariposa War that I will discuss later. The Chowchilla suffered the same fate, as we will see. (Gayton 1948:149, 157, 199).

village subchief, and various occupations like that of a doctor, but also to less important or even temporary roles. The tribal chief, for example, had to be a member of the eagle clan; it was impossible for someone from a different clan to be the tribal chief even for a short time. A temporary social role is exemplified by the caretaker of the sweathouse, who was someone from the bear clan.[9] There was also a spiritual aspect to clans; a totem animal empowered clan members spiritually. Similarly, a person could be shunned or expelled from a clan if that person killed or ate an animal that was a real form of his or her totem. However, an eagle clan member, for example, could keep a juvenile eagle as a "pet" for a short time if it was treated and respected.

In some other native societies, the incest taboo was intimately associated with clan identity and it could be said that the clan was defined by the individuals that are forbidden to marry or have sex with each other, even if the kinship ties are unknown. In contrast, the Chowchilla and other Yuroks and Miwok tribes extended the incest taboo beyond an individual clan to two large groups of clans. Foothill Yokuts called one of these groups the *Tokelyuwich* clans, meaning of the west or downstream clans, and called the other group the *Nutuwich* clans, meaning of the east or upstream clans. Applying the incest taboo, someone in any of the *Tokelyuwich* clans had to marry a person from one of the *Nutuwich* clans. Since the two groups split the tribe into two halves, they are referred to as *moieties* or *exogamous moieties* to empathize the connection with the incest taboo. Chowchilla moieties were also tied to leadership. The tribal chief was the chief of the eagle clan that was part of the *Tokelyuwich* moiety.

The application of the incest taboo to the moieties created additional strength to tribal unity. If an individual in one clan had to marry someone from a different clan there was unity between clans, but the requirement of marrying someone in the opposite moiety locked in unity in the whole tribe. Other rules added more tribal unity. One of these was the rule that a person should marry his or her *patrilateral cross* cousin, i.e., an individual was expected to marry his or her father's sister's child who would be in the opposite moiety. This rule was applied loosely by the Chowchilla people in general but applied especially to the chief's family. If the chief's family did not follow this rule, it would lead to a much larger number of people being eligible to inherit the role of chief and, hence, it would lessen the unity of the society. Other Chowchilla rules were the levirate and the sororate. The

---

9. Gayton 1948:60.

former rule proscribed that, when a man died, his widow was required to marry his brother regardless of whether the brother was already married, and the latter rule was the opposite, namely that when a woman died, her husband was required to marry her sister regardless of whether the sister was already married. Both of these rules changed marriage from an alliance between individuals, families, and clans to an alliance between moieties. Both of these rules were most enforced by public acceptance when they applied to the chief's patrilineage, because a death called into question the reciprocity of the moieties.

You are now beginning to see what it meant to be a Chowchilla in the eighteenth century. In some cases, the parents of a boy and a girl would arrange their marriage early in their lives and the marriage would be consummated when they reached puberty. More commonly, a young man would court a young woman by bringing gifts for her parents. Anthropologists call this a "bride price," but it was not a monetary transaction; the gifts were mainly food meant as an indication that the groom was proposing a durable interfamilial bond and that the woman and her children would be thereafter be part of the groom's family and not of her natal family. This, obviously, provided additional solidarity in the whole tribe. If the gifts were accepted, the marriage was considered set and the young persons would be told whom they were to marry. The girl could refuse a suitor by refusing to accept his gifts, but this was unusual. The couple was later married when the gifts were sufficient and the man was invited to sleep with his bride at her parent's house.[10]

Sex outside of marriage was, of course, looked upon as very disruptive, more so than in most of the world's societies. Before marriage, the girl was watched carefully and always accompanied by a family member to make sure there was no sexual intercourse before formal marriage by gift exchange. Extramarital sex was even more disastrous, of course, for the family, clan, and moiety, and the penalty might be that everyone in the village ostracizes the adulterers. Mayfield tells us that two houses were about 300 yards outside of the Choinumne village where he grew up. In one of the houses lived two women and in the other lived a *berdache*, i.e., a man who lived as a woman. According to Mayfield, unmarried males could visit these houses after dark.[11] Extramarital sex of this sort was apparently condoned.

---

10. The foregoing is based upon Gayton's work among the Chukchansi (Gayton 1948:194–196).

11. Mayfield 1929:107–108; Kroeber 1925:497.

A man could marry outside his own tribe if the marriage restrictions made an acceptable local marriage impossible, but moiety exogamy always applied, because other Yokuts and Miwok tribes had the equivalent of *Nutuwich* and *Tokelyuwich* moieties.[12] Such intertribal marriages were important because they promoted trade and resource sharing and because alliances could be formed for future intertribal problems.

Turning now to Chowchilla leadership, the tribe and each village were led by a village chief, a subchief, and a *winatum*. These people held their leadership positions for life and were replaced only when they died or became incapacitated. As Kroeber pointed out, Chowchilla leaders could be men or women.[13] A woman could lead the village or the whole tribe for the simple reason that she was more capable of leading than any of the men in the eagle lineage at the time of the death of her predecessor. However, because the society placed great emphasis upon patrilineal descent for unity and stability and because such descent was traced through the male line, the leadership usually reverted to a man of the woman's choice when she died. For this reason (and also to avoid the clumsiness of the sexual pronouns in English), I hope I will be forgiven for using masculine pronouns for leaders. As we will see in a later chapter, a time will come when women led the Chowchilla.

A chief, tribal or village, traditionally came from the eagle clan in the *Tokelyuwich* moiety. The other chief, the subchief, probably came from the most important clan in the *Nutuwich* moiety, but, as far as I know, there is no solid evidence of this. During the Mariposa War, there was a Chowchilla chief named Jose Juarez who stepped forward to call for violence against the American invasion, but who was secondary to Jose Rey. His behavior suggests that he was not a dependent of Jose Rey but rather an independent chief representing a different part of the tribe, just as we might expect of a strong leader from the opposite moiety.

The *winatum* was the chief's messenger and was chosen by the chief.[14] The word *messenger*, though, does not capture the importance of the *winatum*, because his main function was to convey and explain the directions of the chief to the people in and around the village. This pattern of leadership elevated the perception of the chief as a wise father figure who guides the village people but does not command them. This was also seen

---

12. Kroeber 1925:493.
13. Kroeber 1925:496.
14. Gayton 1948:148,198.

in the *winatum*'s duties in various ceremonies. The chief was not directly involved in mourning ceremonies, for example; the *winatum* was responsible for announcing mourning ceremonies and directing the preparation of the site. When the ceremony concerned people from other villages, the *winatum* went there to announce the ceremony and tell them when to come.

The headman or headwoman of the largest village was also the tribal chief. The Chowchilla chief had the same responsibilities as the other village headmen, but he or she had greater status and respect, and his or her directions held much greater weight than that of other headmen. Jose Rey was the chief of the Chowchilla before the Mariposa War and maintained the reverence of his people even when incarcerated in the San Juan Bautista Mission. The other Chowchilla leader, Jose Juarez, was with him in the mission and also stepped back into his leadership role despite his prolonged absence.

Since the Chowchilla were patrilineal, one might guess that the succession of the chief's role would tend to be from the chief to his or her eldest son. Actual successions could be from the chief to anyone in the chief's line. The new chief could be one of the chief's brothers or sisters. Also, since all of the preadult generation of a family line called each other brothers and sisters, it was possible for the new chief to emerge from that large group, i.e., be a niece or nephew or a cousin of a niece or nephew. All that is certain was that when a chief died, his or her successor would be someone from the former chief's patrilineal family, clan, and moiety.[15]

According to Kroeber and Gayton's informants,[16] Yokuts people were generally peaceful and wars were rare. There were, of course, occasional incidents at the homeland borders, but these involved individuals and families and rarely escalated to larger groups. When it did escalate to a serious physical confrontation of people representing different tribes, the matter was settled by a duel of champions, not by warriors from one tribe fighting the warriors of another.[17] Typically, two groups from the hostile tribes would meet in an open field and yell insults at each other. Then one man from each tribe would take the role of champion of his tribe and they would fight a duel. The injury or death of one of them would end hostilities, and the losing tribe would withdraw and the winning tribe would take

---

15. Kroeber seems to disagree with this, stating categorically that succession was father to son (Kroeber 1925:496).
16. Kroeber 1925:497; Gayton 1948:176.
17. Gayton 1948:159–160.

land or food resources. When the Chowchilla were fighting the Americans, this way of resolving conflict led to tragedy. During the Mariposa War, a Chowchilla village in which there were people assembled from multiple tribes was attacked by a group of Americans led by James Savage. The native warriors took up positions in the brush or behind rocks where they could shoot arrows without being seen. The Americans similarly took up positions where they could fire their guns without being hit with arrows. During the standoff, native warriors stepped forward one by one to challenge Savage to a duel, only to be slaughtered by the Americans' guns.

Disputes within the tribe normally did not require the intervention of the chief. Within a family, the family leader settled the matter quickly because the family was every person's life and blood. When there were disputes between families in a village, the headman was actively involved, settling disputes in the interests of maintaining village unity.[18] Similarly, the headman did not participate in a death ritual of a family other than his own; the family of the deceased would have the sad ritual and the cremation shortly after death. The headman, on the other hand, was very involved in the annual mourning ceremony given to honor all of the people who had died in the preceding year. He would decide when the ceremony would begin and end and orchestrate the parts of the six-day ceremony.[19] Other responsibilities of a leader included sanctioning family projects and house movements, controlling village spread, arranging activities in which the village as a whole took part (e.g., in deer drives), and directing the building of sweat lodges. The most important function of the leaders, however, was the initiation of the village pilgrimages to collect acorns and salmon.

The ecological relationships between the native people and their acorns and salmon were more complicated than is now commonly thought. Oaks grew throughout the Chowchilla homeland, but, as I mentioned above, the largest and most productive oaks in the Sierras grew at around 1,000 feet in elevation, and it was necessary to go up to that elevation because the number of acorns needed was very large. Acorns were consumed every day at every meal. Many hundreds of pounds of acorns had to be collected for each person and stored in silos such that they lasted until another harvest occurred. All able-bodied people in a village had to go together and camp near good trees, sending women repeatedly down to their village with huge baskets full of acorns on their backs. The acorn harvest was complicated by

---

18. Gayton 1930:378,148.
19. Gayton 1930:199–201; Spier 1978:479–481.

the fact that oaks do not produce the same amount of acorns each year; in some years, all of the black oaks would fail to produce enough acorns. As a consequence, the village headmen had to choose the right time to send his village people into the nearby mountains. Further complicating the headman's decision was the fall salmon run, which would be happening at the same time. Part of the village people had to go to a camping spot on a river to catch and smoke the salmon for storage.[20] In addition, all of the Chowchilla villages had to collect both acorns and salmon at the same time. An important characteristic of a headman or chief was that he could mentally juggle all of the environmental factors in the fall and coordinate their activity with other villages to ensure that there would be enough acorns and salmon to feed everyone in the village for a year. The salmon run in the spring, of course, eased this burden somewhat.

As suggested above, the Yokuts were very concerned about spiritual power and, as all human beings everywhere have done, they sought to explain this power. Their explanations consisted of stories about ancient events, events that were somewhat convoluted and differed from tribe to tribe, but events that were based upon two general beliefs. One of these was that power had always existed and, in the beginning, it had been used by animals to create the world. For the foothills tribes like the Chowchilla, the animals were birds, but birds that acted and communicated with each other as humans did. Gayton and Newman called them "bird people."[21] It is unclear in the Yokuts stories whether or not the bird-people created human beings as well as the earth, but they taught the humans important skills, e.g., how to turn acorns into food. After coexisting with humans for a while, the bird-people decided that they did not want to live as humans did and they flew away. Before they left, Eagle, the bird-people leader, named and transformed some of the bird-people into animals—coyote, cougar, fox, bear, owl, skunk, and others—that would stay with the humans and would have some residual power. The other general belief was that the power left behind, although concentrated in animals, is also found in other living things and objects in nature, and that the power is mobile. Human beings can gain power by fasting and dreaming about their totem animals and asking them for power in the form of some skill. Commonly, this was healing power, but it could be any kind of power.

---

20. The number of places along the rivers at which a group of people could camp and catch salmon was limited. Except at certain spots on the riverbanks, tule bulrushes grew thickly and made it impossible to reach the water, just as they do today.
21. Gayton and Newman 1940:39.

The Chowchilla, like their neighbors, had two important rituals: the annual mourning ritual mentioned above and the Jimsonweed ritual. The first of these helped people shed their grief for deceased relatives and gave them an opportunity to send useful things that the deceased relative might need in the afterlife by burning their things in a great fire. This ritual was focused upon family relationships rather than upon individuals.

In contrast, the Jimsonweed ceremony was done by individuals specifically to gain personal spiritual power, if only for a brief time. This ritual was held in the spring and anyone, male or female, could participate. Commonly, the participants were either young people entering adulthood or people of any age concerned about illness. If a person or a person's relative was ill, drinking the Jimsonweed might be done to determine the cause or the remedy of the illness, and if the visions received were very strong, a person could become a Jimsonweed doctor. Participation in the ritual was by no means mandatory. Established doctors commonly participated each year, but other individuals chose whether or not to take part. Jimsonweed was very dangerous and could kill a person if, they believed, he or she inadvertently performed the ritual improperly. For example, the person did not fast appropriately or participated at times other than spring. Consequently, there were members of the tribe who, having witnessed serious negative effects upon others, feared the Jimsonweed and refused to take it.

The ritual began with participants fasting for eight days. This meant that they would eat no meat for six days and then eat nothing at all for two days. During this time, the participants were expected to meditate and mentally beseech the Jimsonweed to provide strong visions. While this was happening, a Jimsonweed doctor went out to collect the plant. This usually entailed multiple days because the plant did not grow everywhere. The best Jimsonweed was thought to grow along the Fresno River in Chowchilla territory.[22]

On the morning after the fasting ended, the old man brought out the plants he had gathered and announced the ritual by running around the village two or three times. He then crushed the plant's root with a *mano* and *metate* (mortar and pestle) and put the mashed plant in a cooking basket with water to extract the juice. Later that day, when he judged the extract was strong enough, he gathered the participants and administered the extract to each, taking into consideration factors such as the age and weight of each person. The effect of the potion was immediate and the

---

22. Gayton 1948:211.

participants began dancing. In a short time, each of them fell into a stupor and was dragged to a spot where he or she could be watched through the night. The next morning, the participants would begin having hallucinations that were unique to each person but generally associated with the reason the participant had taken the potion. The hallucinations stopped after a few days and the participant then freely told others what he or she had seen and learned. Having thus established that he or she had received meaningful and useful power, the participant would thereafter be considered to be a person who could use Jimsonweed spiritual power, for specific purposes or general well-being.

Jimsonweed ceremonies had the subtle, positive function of social cohesion. People who had taken the potion were considered strong, useful people. In threatening situations, they were expected to come forward to fight the illness or the enemy. The only potentially negative social effect of taking the potion lay in the accumulation of power in doctors, because it was believed that doctors could harm people as well as help people. Further, a strong malevolent doctor did not have to be very near his[23] target; he could deliver a disease or a poison through the air to his victim. This made doctors unreliable and fearful rather than respected. We can only speculate about the natives' explanation of epidemics that arrived with the Spanish or Americans, even though there was no direct contact.

---

23. Most were male.

3

Spanish Destruction

We now turn to the earliest instigators of change, the Spanish. They had been in Mexico and had explored the perimeter of California for more than two centuries, but in the 1760s they decided that the time had come to claim and inhabit the coastal land to the north. In 1769, the invasion began with platoons of soldiers, each with a few priests, sent north with the mission of building forts (presidios) and churches at strategic locations along the coast of California. The presidio, church, and associated buildings at each location were subsequently identified as an independent mission. Today more than a million Americans visit the missions each year and are told that the constructions were the work of saintly and altruistic Franciscan priests. The priests are thus given credit for building the missions, farming the land, and introducing domestic animals; when the visitors leave, they are sure that the Spaniards were very constructive people who built something out of nothing. The reality, however, is quite different. First, the native people built the missions, and all of the labor associated with the missions was performed through the coercion of native people. Second and more significant, the Spaniards were much more destructive than they were constructive. When the missions were finally secularized and divested of their duty to convert native people to Catholicism in the 1830s, all that remained were the crumbling remnants of structures built by their cruel exploitation of the native people and the aftermath of their colossal ecological blunders.

The primary purpose of the missions was not to spread Christianity but to demonstrate Spanish ownership of the Pacific coast north of Mexico. In the 1760s, news had reached Mexico City that Russian and British fur trappers were moving into that area. This alarmed the Spanish government in Mexico. They accurately predicted that the countries represented by the beaver and seal hunters would try to gain control of the land north of Mexico and that, ultimately, those governments would become a threat to Mexico.[1] It was therefore necessary to send soldiers up the coastline to protect "their" land. However, the Spanish army in Mexico at that time was weak and poorly equipped, and there were heavy demands from Spain for royal tributes. The central government could not afford to adequately supply and resupply garrisons at a distance from the capital. To overcome these limits, the leaders in Mexico City changed the military expedition to resemble their forces when they conquered Central America two centuries earlier. A cadre of priests would march north with the soldiers. The military would establish presidios along the coast of California while the priests would subdue the natives and convince them that growing food in support of the garrisons was their natural role in the Spanish empire. This was a gamble; the garrisons would not be able to protect the coast and grow food at the same time. In any case, the soldiers were uneducated young men from the lowest class in Mexico City with little or no knowledge of farming.[2] If the natives in the north could not be forced to grow food for the soldiers, the expedition would be a failure; the coast would remain unprotected. Thus, from the very beginning, the plans of the expedition included using the soldiers to make peons of the native people and to employ whatever force was necessary to maintain them in that condition. Converting them to Catholicism would be a possible but not essential part of the expedition. The important thing to do was to make farmers out of the natives as quickly as possible.

This proved to be a difficult task, much more difficult than what the Spaniards had encountered in Mexico. The villagers in Mexico were farmers under the control of an urban aristocracy long before the Spaniards arrived.[3] The native people that the expedition found in California were hunters and gatherers whose villages were not permanently located and who had a meager knowledge, if any, of horticulture. It was therefore necessary to use different and more violent methods. Thus, after the invasion of the northern coast had been going on for four years and five missions had been built from San Diego to Carmel, the most senior priest among of

1. Jackson and Castillo 1995:27.
2. Cook 1960:241.
3. Spencer and Jennings 1965:467–468, 470–472.

the priests in the north went to Mexico City and made an appeal to the government for the adoption of a more forceful approach to converting natives to farming. This priest, Junipero Serra, proposed that the central purpose of the missions be shifted to proselytization and that his priests be given the authority to use corporal punishment in their work of converting and controlling natives.[4] Both a military officer and a priest would lead soldiers sent out to native villages. The priest would withhold baptism from the natives and, glorifying the benefits of Catholicism with heavily armed soldiers standing behind him, recommend that the natives go to the missions.[5] Once inside the missions, the priests could command the soldiers to divest the natives of their primitive culture by using punishments of flogging, solitary confinement, mutilation, use of stocks, branding, and even execution to quell any resistance.[6]

The Spanish government in Mexico City quickly approved Serra's proposal in 1773 and, in the next 27 years, 13 new missions had to be added to the five previously established missions to hold all of the captured native people. Each of the 18 missions held several hundred natives by 1800.[7] This was important because it was impossible for the small number of priests at each mission to deal with numbers of that size. The priests thus had to rely upon the military to force the natives to raise crops and to enforce the priests' edict that the captives must live pure lives in accordance to the Catholic moral code. The priests would baptize natives, give them Spanish names, and carefully list them as neophytes in the mission's records. Thereafter, the soldiers took charge, reducing the captives to slaves and driving them as if they were herds of animals. To ensure that there was no premarital sex, unmarried men and women were separated and locked up at night in large, crowded barracks that had neither water nor toilets. Natives were not allowed to behave in any manner that reflected their traditional cultures and could be harshly punished if they did. Even their native names and tribal identities were forbidden. Many years later, two Chowchilla chiefs, Jose Rey and Jose Juarez, returned to their homeland bearing Spanish names and were subsequently known only by those names.

---

4. Jackson and Castillo 1995:27.
5. This is amply demonstrated by numerous reports about later forays by priests and military leaders. See Cook 1960:239–292.
6. Castillo 1978:101.
7. Jackson and Castillo 1995:53–56. By 1820, the number of incarcerated natives in 20 missions reached 21,000.

The soldiers, however, were not required to live moral lives. They were indispensable and, consequently, all immoral or criminal outrages perpetrated against native people by soldiers were disregarded. This gave the soldiers license to grossly mistreat, injure, and even kill natives for no reason, without censure or penalties. Soldiers who had contagious diseases were separated from other soldiers but not from natives. Disease became a constant in the lives of all of the natives as a result of their lack of immunity to European infections. Epidemics of diphtheria, pneumonia, measles, dysentery, and tuberculosis swept through the missions, leading to high death rates among the natives.[8] Five to ten percent of the adults died each year and the death rate for children was as high as 33 percent in some years.[9] Native women were attacked and raped with impunity. Rape was a form of recreation for the soldiers. The woman and her family, especially if newly arrived and baptized, would be badly traumatized but revenge invited more torture. If the rape had occurred in a traditional Yokuts culture, the woman's family and clan would have had the right and obligation to kill the assailant. In addition, the chances of getting syphilis from a soldier were high, and this fate would give a raped woman a painful life and an early death. Partly because it was possible for an individual to have the disease without showing symptoms, syphilis spread within the missions to native men, women, and children. Eventually, syphilis became the most common cause of death in the missions as a whole.[10] Sadly, escaped natives spread the disease to free native populations beyond the missions. We do not know whether syphilis reached the Chowchilla, but, considering the thousands of Yokuts captured and taken to missions, it seems unlikely that the disease was not transmitted to some of them.

After Serra died in 1784, the missions slowly began to change their nature. The priests and soldiers continued to capture native people, but at a somewhat slower rate. One possible reason for this slowdown was that the expeditions sent out to capture native people had to go longer distances. All of the Yokuts villages in the flat portion of the San Joaquin Valley had been raided, making it necessary to go into the Sierra foothills where the Chowchilla and other Yokuts tribes lived. Another reason might have been that the missions were becoming too large for the relatively small number of priests to operate. As I mentioned above, each mission had several hundred captured natives at the end of the eighteenth century.

8. Cook 1976a:13–34.
9. Cook 1976a:424.
10. Cook 1976a:22.

In the late years of that century, food shortages became common, and famine threatened the existence of some missions. The number of natives working in the fields was large and increasing, but they could not produce enough food. The fault, however, did not lie in the size of the workforce but in the ineptitude of the priests and soldiers. Mistakes were constantly made, followed by stopgap, emergency measures taken to make up the difference in production. They did not plan for vagaries in the weather. In some years there was drought, and in others the rain came at the wrong time. Adequate irrigation was impossible without dams to store the water for distribution when needed. What was most important, however, was that in addition to causing famine conditions, the missions caused the wholesale destruction of the environment, destruction that would haunt the tribes and undermine their cultures, destruction that continues to degrade the quality of life for everyone living in the San Joaquin Valley today.

In brief, the Spaniards stripped large areas for cultivation but failed to fertilize the fields.[11] As the fertility of the soil diminished in cultivated fields, new fields had to be developed farther from the mission. Some mission fields were as much as 20 miles from the mission.[12] They simultaneously imported livestock from Mexico and Spain and developed large herds of cattle, horses, sheep, and pigs that were left unattended beyond the cultivated fields. So prolific were these animals that by 1800 there were 50,000 cattle, 86,000 sheep, and 11,000 horses running wild in the San Joaquin Valley.[13] The number and effects of the pigs has not, to my knowledge, been fully studied, but they gravitated to the oak forests and ate large quantities of the acorns that sustained small animals and birds, as well as the native people. A single full-grown pig can consume in one day all of the acorns produced in one year. All of this livestock displaced many of the animals that were food resources for the native people, but, strangely, they did not add appreciably to the food supply of the crowded missions. The deer, antelopes, and tulle elk herds on the wide, open flatlands of the Valley were easy to scare but difficult to hunt. Perhaps the new livestock were also hard to catch. In any case, the new grazing animals drove the native animals out by consuming the native bunch grass and preventing its regrowth. Bunch grass grows seeds at the tops of its stems and, consequently, when those were eaten, the plants could not reproduce. Further,

---

11. Castillo 1978:100; Jackson and Castillo 1995:6–7.
12. Cook 1943:75.
13. Jackson and Castillo 1995:123–131.

each bunch grass plant grew to six feet across and offered shelter and food for insects, birds, and small mammals.

The destruction by the new livestock was compounded by the fact that the animals carried the seeds of invasive weeds from Mexico and Spain tangled in their fur or in their stomachs. Invasive plants, like thistles, took the places of native plants, crowding out species such as clover, wild potatoes, and wild tomatoes that the native people ate, and yet other plants that they used for medicine and basketry. One of the plants, in particular, was catastrophically invasive. Botanists tell us that 99 percent of the grass in California today is the bottom-growing grass that came from Spain at the time of the missions,[14] and while this grass offered some advantages, it was particularly destructive because it grew and filled the space under the bunch grass before the bunch grass seeds were produced in the spring. As a consequence, grass was instrumental in causing the ecologies of the land to collapse, and it was such collapses that made it impossible for native people to regain their traditional lifestyle.

The changing environment was apparent to the Chowchilla before soldiers came across the San Joaquin. The disappearance of the deer, antelope, and elk herds out on the flatlands deprived the native people of a significant source of food, and the appearance of wild pigs in the oak forests was strange and worrisome. The men could hunt the new animals but it changed things. Horses were more dangerous than the deer or antelopes. The men who knew how to corral deer were not important anymore. Still, the horses were bigger than most of the animals the Chowchilla hunted; horses fed more people and tasted good to them. The villages were marked by large heaps of horse bones, but this was good; the people were happy with so much meat. But then came the rumors that native people were taken away and not allowed to go back to their villages. And there was great sickness where they were taken.

To the Chowchilla people listening to escapees, it must have seemed that disease and death would be waiting for them when they were pushed through the gates of a mission. In general, unfortunately, this was true. The missions' unsanitary conditions gave all of the missions a relatively high death rate, averaging about 75 deaths per year per 1,000 natives. But the threat to their health differed from mission to mission, from year to year, and, most likely, from month to month. Some of the diseases (e.g., syphilis and tuberculosis) steadily added to the death rate, but others diseases (e.g.,

---

14. Stromberg et al. 2002.

Figure 5. Earliest known drawing of San Juan Bautista mission, dated 1847.
Courtesy David McLaughlin.

influenza, pneumonia, measles, diphtheria, cholera, tetanus, and salmonellosis) struck suddenly and killed many natives in a short time, which could easily increase the death rate for a particular year to be above 100 for a given mission. This would be an increase in deaths of more than 30 percent. Epidemics can be identified in the records when disease caused significant deaths in more than half of the missions in the same year.[15]

Expeditions—i.e., attacks upon native villages for the purpose of capturing more slaves for the missions—were most common after epidemics occurred, but the priests no doubt still put pressure upon the presidios to send troops out after a nonepidemic disease occurred with a high death rate. The latter cases were much more numerous in the records than epidemics. For example, at Mission San Juan Bautista, the mission to which Chowchilla people were commonly taken, 13 of the 38 years that the mission existed had high death rates similar to epidemic rates, but only 5 years of the 13 appear to have been epidemics.[16] At that mission, consequently, the demand by priests for more raids by the soldiers stationed there tended to happen every third year on average, but larger expeditions, with soldiers from multiple missions going together, tended to occur every nine years. This suggests that, if you were a Chowchilla, the chances of your whole village being taken to this mission were 5/38, or about one in eight, but the chances of you getting a potentially fatal disease were 13/38, or about one in three.

---

15. Being easily communicated and therefore widespread, epidemic diseases probably killed many nonmission natives, but records of this are missing.
16. Jackson and Castillo 1995:135.

Figure 6. Drawing of San Juan Bautista mission by Edward Vischer in 1872.
Courtesy of David McLaughlin.

Some of the expeditions were deceptively nonviolent. In 1804, a priest named Juan Martin went to a Yokuts village near the Tulare Lake and, with armed soldiers behind him, asked the villagers to *give* him their "little sons." The soldiers persuaded the priest not to kidnap the children, not because they thought it was wrong, and not because it was a shocking and incredibly inhumane thing to do, but because it would be difficult to take all 200 of the children in the village.[17]

The expeditions that went out from San Juan Bautista and entered Chowchilla Territory began in 1806, when Lieutenant Gabriel Moraga and Father Fray Pedro Muñez took a troop of 25 soldiers from Mission San Juan Bautista to locate native villages beyond the San Joaquin River.[18] This was one of the first forays by Moraga, who would go on to lead numerous attacks on native villages.[19]

Shortly after reaching the San Joaquin River, Moraga and Muñez were met by 42 warriors and taken to a Nupchenchi village, probably Copicha, which was on the east side of the San Joaquin across from the mouth of the Chowchilla River. As I mentioned above, the Nupchenchi shared salmon

17. Cook 1960:243.
18. Cook 1960:247–254.
19. Ultimately, Moraga would make 46 such attacks, more than any other officer of the Spanish army and all in a period of 12 years (1805 through 1817).

fishing with the Chowchilla and were consequently allies of the Chowchilla. Since Moraga arrived at the river on September 25, it was likely that some of the people who greeted him were Chowchilla. In any case, the people at that location welcomed the Spaniards and performed the Yokuts traditional welcome ceremony, showering the visitors with grass seed.

Several days later, Moraga's party found themselves confronted by 79 warriors as they approached the Merced River from the north. Here again, Moraga's party was taken to their village on the south side of the river and welcomed with the seed sprinkling ceremony. In return, Moraga and Muñez thought it only right to invite them to become Catholics so that they could be friends. This was a deceptive invitation, of course; they made it clear that the native people had to be baptized to be friends, and, after baptizing a few very old people, they told the native people that they would have to go to a mission to be baptized. Early the next year, Moraga returned to Yokuts territory with 25 men to capture native people for the missions and, specifically, to recapture escaped neophytes.[20] On that trip, he planned to start at the south end of the valley and sweep through villages going north. However, the Tulamni Yokuts attacked his expedition near Bakersfield, killing two of his men and stealing 100 of his horses. Moraga consequently had to skip the villages he had seen the previous year and return to Mission San Jose empty-handed.[21]

Thereafter, the expeditions into the Central Valley became more violent. On larger, falsely evangelical expeditions, soldiers brutally marched village populations to missions.[22] These expeditions were not always successful, though. In 1815, for example, a Spanish force arrived at the south side of the San Joaquin River, coincidentally at exactly the same location where Moraga's party had been nine years earlier, at Copicha. In this case, however, the intention of the Spanish was not in any way peaceful. The Chowchilla had been successfully raiding the farms at Mission San Juan Bautista for three years,[23] and there is little doubt that the Spanish soldiers had been sent to capture or kill whatever Chowchilla people they could find. With superior weapons, the Spanish were sure of doing just that. However, Chowchilla warriors had been forewarned and rushed to meet the soldiers

---

20. Baptized natives.
21. Cook 1960:255.
22. Cook 1960:267. Data supporting this statement lie in the expedition descriptions gathered in Cook (1960 and 1962).
23. Cook 1960:190.

at the Nupchenchi village.[24] When the Spaniards arrived, a volley of arrows shot across the river startled the soldiers and, instead of crossing the river, they retreated and did not stop retreating until they were five miles from the river. The soldiers reassembled there and, after considering the situation further, the officers decided to go back and cross the river at dawn, thereby conquering the native warriors with a surprise attack. When the first light of dawn came, however, the Spaniards found that the Chowchilla warriors had surrounded them. Wanting to save his soldiers, the Spanish officer, Jose Pico, went out and nonchalantly claimed that he meant them no harm and asked them what they wanted. The Chowchilla immediately replied that they had come to fight and began shooting arrows. The Spaniards loaded their muskets, but, before they could fire, the Chowchilla disappeared into the underbrush where they could fire their arrows without being seen. The Spanish saw they were trapped and pushed through the circle of warriors, taking three captives as they fled, claiming victory.[25]

Such face-to-face battles were relatively uncommon. Knowing that the Spaniards could kill someone at a much greater distance than they could shoot an arrow, the Chowchilla, as well as other Yokuts, would simply disappear into the underbrush and wait until they left. During the Mexican Period (1821–1846), this was the only way that a village could survive. In 1828, Sebastian Rodriguez led a small army to kill natives, thought to be horse thieves, living on the east side of the San Joaquin. When the army arrived there, Rodriguez broke it into platoons that would go to different areas. Corporal Simeon Castro was chosen to take a force of 17 soldiers and 16 neophytes to attack all villages in the Chowchilla homeland. Rodriguez must have been shocked when he heard that Corporal Simeon "had not encountered a single Indian in Chowchilla country."[26]

From 1828 to 1834, however, the number of native raids upon farms and ranchos and the amount of livestock taken in these raids increased steadily.[27] This was caused by the proliferation of wild horses in the Valley, as I have mentioned above, but also by beaver hunting, which I will explain in the next chapter. However, multiple problems emerged with this switch

---

24. The Nupchenchi people had hidden themselves in the tules two days earlier, possibly because they knew that there would be a battle at Copicha. Also, the Chowchilla warriors were nearby because, as mentioned before, they came to collect salmon. This fight took place on Nov. 10, 1815, when the fall salmon run was still going on.
25. Cook 1960:268–269.
26. Cook 1962:185.
27. Cook 1960:190.

in diet. The time and energy required in killing a wild horse and transporting the meat to the village was much greater than doing the same with
a local deer. The Chowchilla and other Yokuts soon discovered that taking
tame horses from the corrals of farms and ranches was much easier, and
had the added benefits of crippling work on the Spaniards' ranches and
farms and undermining the Spanish effort to expand their territory into
the California interior.[28]

The Chowchilla, in particular, became very adept at taking tame horses.
A group of seven or more warriors would set out on foot and walk day and
night across the San Joaquin Valley and over the Coast Range to the Spanish
ranchos and missions. Once there, they looked for horses kept in corrals
and chose a target. Then, after the priests and ranchers had gone to sleep,
they quietly opened the corrals and let the horses walk out by themselves.
Some distance from the corral, they would mount some of the horses and
drive the herd east, taking a circuitous route and reversing the direction of
the herd to confuse any pursuers. This involved expert horsemanship, but
the trip back to the villages was made easier by the fact that tame horses
will run as a herd. Untamed horses were more likely to scatter. Even tame
horses tended to spread out when the herd was traveling at a gallop, so the
Chowchilla modified certain of their arrows so that the arrowhead would
penetrate the horses' skin but no deeper. These arrows were as effective
as a whip in keeping all of the horses together.[29] At mountain passes and
arroyos, they would leave a few warriors to ambush the pursuers by firing
arrows from hiding, and, since pursuers could not tell how many native
men lay in ambush, this was usually effective in dissuading further pursuit.

The priests and ranchers, of course, became irate at the loss of their
animals and sent riders after the horses, even though this was not rational.
First, there were unbelievably large herds of wild horses in the Valley, and
it was easier to catch and break horses than to track down and recover
stolen tame horses. In addition, riders sent out were likely to find that
the horses had been killed and the meat laid out to dry in the sun before
they were found. In addition, tame animals were plentiful in the Mexican
towns.[30] Richard Dana, who visited California in 1834, tells us in his book,
Two Years Before the Mast, that the Mexicans treated horses almost as a
throwaway commodity. If someone borrowed a horse, it did not much

---

28. Cook 1976a:229; Castillo 1978:106.
29. Gayton 1948:183–184; Phillips 1993:102–104.
30. Phillips 1993:76.

matter if the horse was not returned as long as the saddle was returned.[31] Much of the anger concerning stolen horses could be explained by the growing stratification of Mexican society. Ranchers and priests measured their status by the number of horses and cattle they owned.[32] The theft of horses by the native people was seen as an insult, an affront to their status. The Chowchilla and their neighbors were considered loathsome, immoral criminals, as if they, the Mexicans, were innocent and peaceful citizens who had no responsibility in the matter.[33] And, because they had high status in the towns and at the missions, they demanded that the government send soldiers to capture and punish the natives.

When military action was initiated in this way, the emphasis was always on punishing the natives, not capturing them; the soldiers would savagely kill any or all men, women, and children in a village that had horses or had what was left of the horses.[34] To demonstrate that they had fulfilled their orders, they cut off the ears of their victims to take back to headquarters. In 1834, a group of American trappers was camping in the Sierra foothills when a platoon of Mexican soldiers arrived with cannons. They told the Americans that a sizable group of natives, presumably a village, had been captured and taken to Mission San Juan Bautista, but the natives had then escaped with 300 horses. The soldiers were then ordered to go out again and bring the horses back and punish the natives. The soldiers had found some natives that they thought were the escapees on a nearby mountain, but they were afraid to attack because, judging from the campfire smoke coming from the natives' village, they thought there were a very large number of natives. The Mexicans then proposed that, if the Americans helped attack, the Americans could have half of the horses. After reaching the base of the mountain, the Mexicans set up their cannons and fired them at the natives' campfire smoke. This apparently did nothing but warn the natives of their approach, and when the Mexicans and Americans entered the village, most of the natives were gone. Only elderly people and very young children who could not escape remained. There were mission horses there, but most of them had been butchered. It was clear that nothing was gained in the attack and the Mexicans flew into a rage and proceeded to mercilessly slaughter all of the old people and children and cut off their ears to take back and show to the rancheros and officers. The Mexicans pushed some of

31. Dana 1840:73, 108.
32. Phillips 1993:107.
33. Latta 1949:33–34; Phillips 1993:107–116.
34. Cook 1962:202–203.

the defenseless natives into a house, barricaded the door, and piled wood around the house, intending to burn the house and kill all of those inside. The Americans stopped this and released the people in the house, only to see the Mexicans massacre them all.[35]

The accounts in Cook's collection[36] show us that Mexican ranchers and farmers were also affected by this incredible, sickening ethnic insanity. When addressing the problem of horse stealing, they went out to kill whatever natives they happened to find. Jose Amador, who had a farm near Danville, took several trips to San Joaquin Valley to find natives to kill. In 1837, he and a group of other native-hating men captured 100 Christian Yokuts. Because some Miwok natives told him that the Christian Yokuts were guilty of a heinous crime, Amador executed six of them every half mile as they marched along.

The era of Spanish destruction in California finally came to a close in the late 1830s amidst this gory insanity. It started to end in 1833, when the government in Mexico City proclaimed that the missions must ultimately be secular, as was promised by royal decree when they were started. The Franciscan priests could keep the missions as parishes, but all of the land around the missions was to be given back to the indigenous people. But, of course, there was great resistance from the priests. After all, there was much wrangling in Mexican politics and the argument over secularization was still going on. Nevertheless, secularization proceeded. The first missions to close were in southern California, while priests in more northerly missions stalled for as much as four years. Even then, the missions' outlying farms that could not function without native people working on them continued to disobey the government for a time. As a result, some Chowchilla people were among the last to walk free out of the mission gates.

The return of friends and relatives to the homeland brought great happiness throughout the villages, even though some of the returnees brought new sickness from the missions, as we will see. Most important and most joyful for the Chowchilla was the return of the revered chief of the tribe, Jose Rey, and another strong village chief, Jose Juarez, who had been incarcerated together in a mission. Unfortunately, we have no direct information about how they were captured or about their mission experiences. There is, however, an intriguing report about a Mexican expedition in the late 1830s against a village of native people located in the northern Yokuts foothills,

---

35. Leonard 1839, reproduced in 1934:189–191.
36. Cook 1962:186–203.

an area that included the Chowchilla homeland. This report is about a chief that the Mexicans labeled Domingo, a curious name because native men were given Spanish names when they were baptized at a mission, but the report indicates that this chief was not baptized before the expedition.

The person writing about the expedition was its leader, a man named Innocent Garcia. Garcia spoke the Yokuts language and was living among the Yokuts when he received an order from Juan Alvarado, the Mexican Governor of California.[37] Although he does not write about his own background, it is apparent that he was formerly an officer in the Mexican army because Alvarado's order was to assemble an army and capture a notorious chief named Domingo, who was raiding ranches and farms. Garcia must have had good relations with the Yokuts because he was able to recruit 300 warriors from five different Yokuts tribes, including the chief of each tribe, and assemble them at the junction of the San Joaquin and Kings Rivers in two weeks.[38] A force of Mexican soldiers met Garcia's army there. From the junction, the combined army marched up the San Joaquin River and then turned north into hilly country.[39] The trip required three days of all-day riding but, at some point in the trip, Garcia discovered that it was the Mexican soldiers' intent to attack as they usually did, violently and showing no mercy. He and his chiefs appear to have stopped the march and insist that the Mexican soldiers go back, because Garcia's army went on alone. When they reached Domingo's village, the five chiefs evaluated the geography and then stated that they would proceed only if Garcia let them organize and carry out the attack. Garcia agreed and the five tribal chiefs quietly and carefully arranged their men around the village during the night. At dawn the next day, a war cry was given to waken the village and, finding himself surrounded, Domingo was forced to surrender. All of the people in the village were taken prisoner and no one was killed or wounded.

---

37. Since Alvarado served as governor for only a single year, this expedition must have occurred in 1837.

38. The Kings River does not now flow into the San Joaquin as it did some centuries ago, but in a year with heavy downpours, some of the water from the Kings River goes to the San Joaquin through the Fresno Slough. In the next chapter, I will offer an explanation for the shift in the Kings River drainage.

39. Since magnetic declinations were not known at that time, this would be northwest on modern maps rather than north. Garcia does not give any further indication about the location of Domingo's village, but states that it was remote. This is likely to mean that it was not in the flatlands or in the low rolling hills but in the difficult higher hills.

Domingo's people were marched to Mission San Juan Bautista, where they were divided into three groups. One group consisted of neophytes from Mission San Miguel and a second group consisted of neophytes from Mission San Antonio. These groups were sent back to their respective missions. The remainder, composed of those never baptized, was the largest group. That group was further divided with women in one group and men in another. The women were taken to Mission San Carlos at Carmel while the men were taken to a mission farm near San Juan Bautista. At the farm, Garcia informs us that the men worked diligently in the fields for a substantial period of time. When the time was right, Domingo took some horses and retrieved the women from Carmel and then, returning to the farm, he and his men rounded up all the farm's horses and cattle and drove them back to his village in the high Sierra foothills, leaving not a single horse or cow at the farm. On the way home, Domingo stopped at the village of one of the chiefs who was responsible for his capture and killed the chief's brother to warn other Yokuts tribes not to go against him.[40]

It is possible that Domingo and Jose Rey were the same person and that Jose Rey's followers modified the Spanish name given to him at the mission by adding the Spanish word for *king*. In any case, Jose Rey returned from San Juan Bautista when secularization was finally completed about 1838, and his village was back in the foothills, like Domingo's. The description of the path that Garcia's army of Yokuts followed to Domingo's village would be very similar to a description of the path to Jose Rey's village that was used twelve years later by the vigilantes of the Mariposa War. One thing that can be said is that Jose Rey's stature as leader of the Chowchilla matches that described for Domingo. However, without more evidence, the equation of the two men must remain speculation. At the least, Domingo's story corroborates the strength and centralizing nature of Chowchilla leadership that was evident in Jose Rey during the Mariposa War.

---

40. Cook 1962:198–199.

4

Beaver Trappers
and Epidemics

While the Chowchilla were fighting enemies that attacked them from the west, another threat appeared from the north and east. Fur trappers began to enter the Sierra foothills in large numbers in the 1820s looking for beaver pelts. In retrospect, it can be seen that this invasion was inevitable. A long time before trappers arrived, hat manufacturers in the eastern United States and Europe had discovered that the inner layer of a beaver's hair made an excellent insulator for headwear,[1] and competition between hat makers caused the value of such pelts to become higher and higher. The Pilgrims in Massachusetts recognized the profit in trapping and began collecting pelts as soon as they arrived in 1620. Eventually, the immigrants killed all of the beavers in Massachusetts, so trappers moved west, killing beavers as they moved across the continent. In 1820, it is estimated that hundreds of millions of beavers had been killed in the United States and Canada and virtually all of the remaining beavers were in California.[2]

The man who perpetrated this slaughter in California was John Jacob Astor, the owner of the British Hudson Bay Company. Astor saw that the value of beaver pelts was so high that many trappers would be coming west, and he wanted to get all of California's pelts before anyone else could get them. He first raised the amount he would pay for each pelt above that paid

---

1. Beavers have two layers of hair in their fur. The outer layer is a luxuriant dark brown hair that could have been used for coats. However, the hat manufacturers threw that away and only used the layer of hair nearest the animal's skin. This hair forms an insulating layer, allowing the animals to live through winters in ice-cold water. Hat makers in the era of stovepipe hats and elaborate military headdresses would pay dearly for the pelts. Hurtado 1988:41–42; Wishart 1979:27.
2. Wishart 1979.

by other companies so that he could attract and hire enough trappers to grab all of the beavers in California as fast as possible. To further encourage men to abandon other jobs and go to California for him, he even arranged for trappers to take their families with them, and by 1830 he was sending large parties of men, women, and children into the Sacramento and San Joaquin Valleys. It is clear that Astor wanted to cause the extinction of beavers in California, regardless of any repercussions, and he almost did.

Now, looking back, we can see how incredibly damaging the beaver slaughter was to the lives of the Chowchilla and other native people in the Sierra foothills. When beavers created ponds with their dams, the streams and rivers were transformed into a chain of ponds from the high Sierra down to the Central Valley. Around each pond, the beavers' activities pushed back the forest, creating open sunlit grasslands, littered with the remnants of the beavers' work but ideal for deer and other animals to graze. The ponds themselves were deep, still water, attracting large, diverse populations of insects, fish, reptiles, and birds. In the fall, ducks and geese came to the ponds in great numbers. Deer and elk multiplied, feeding in the grasslands.[3] Native people were also attracted to the resources of the ponds and became an integral part of the ecology. Food was plentiful there and they found plants for medicine and basketry that were scarce elsewhere, partly because invasive Spanish plants crowded them out at lower altitudes.

Then came the beaver trappers, killing the one animal that was at the center of the complex web of interdependencies of plants and animals that we now call the pond ecology. Ponds dried up as the beaver dams failed, and every living thing in the pond ecology had to relocate and establish new dependencies. If this was not possible, the plant or animal died with the beavers. Those that suffered the most, however, were the Chowchilla and other native people, because they had become dependent upon many different pond plants and animals that were directly dependent upon the beavers' work.

It is not possible to describe here all of the ways that killing the beavers affected the Chowchilla. However, one destroyed ecological relationship that was important was the relationship between the beavers and plants known as the tule.[4] Tules are shallow-water plants that grow in marshes

---

3. According to a recent study, the density of the deer residing in the area around beaver dams was four times larger than in nearby forest or chaparral areas (Heizer and Elsasser 1980:73).

4. The full name of this plant is tule bulrush, but the native people use *tule* (pronounced *two-lee*) for both a single plant and groups of plants.

Figure 7. Ash Slough marshland near Chowchilla River swollen by spring runoff. Heavy growth of tules at right prevents access by fishermen.

and along the edges of the streams, rivers, and lakes in the Chowchilla homeland. They are tall, cane-like plants with intertwined rhizomic roots that make them very difficult to uproot. They are also very invasive and grow together so thickly that they completely block humans and most animals from reaching the water. They have some useful characteristics; native people are able to use them for house and raft construction and for medicine made from the pith of the plant. But tules are abhorred for two reasons: They multiply quickly, and the only sections of a river or stream that can be used for fishing are the sections that have rapidly moving currents capable of dislodging the tules. There are lakes of still water in the Sierra foothills that are completely surrounded by tules and cannot be fished at all. Tules are also abhorred because they gradually expand the sloughs (marshes) that are common in Chowchilla territory near the San Joaquin River. In a slough, the tules slow down the water entering from feeder streams and thus cause the water to drop any sediment it is carrying, rather than allowing the sediment to continue downstream. This gives the plant more area to grow and enlarges the slough while decreasing the amount of usable space of the homeland.

Beavers, however, kept the tules in check in multiple ways. First, although they seem to prefer willows, beavers can consume the tules and use them in building their dams and homes. Although the water in beaver ponds is slow moving water, the water is deep because the beavers excavate mud and stones gathered from the bottom of the pond to build their dams. Sediments from upstream continue to enter the pond, but they settle to the bottom where tules cannot use them. However, when the beavers are killed, the dams are washed away and the sediments in the pond are swept downstream to be caught by the tules at lower altitudes. As a result, ponds without beavers at those lower altitudes gradually fill up with tules and become impenetrable marshes. In this way, two large lakes in the southern Yokuts area, Tulare Lake and Buena Vista Lake, became huge marsh areas filled with tules.

In short, the tules and beavers can be said to have a "seesaw" ecological connection. The more beavers there are, the fewer the tules. Kill all of the beavers and the tules increase, taking more land and resources from the Chowchilla homeland. And this is but one of the many ecological connections associated with the complicated pond ecology.[5]

Trappers were also associated with another great catastrophe that fell upon the native people. Around 1830, a ship coming from a tropical land sailed up the Columbia River carrying sailors infected with malaria. Two years later, malaria had become rampant among natives and nonnatives along the Columbia, but John Jacob Astor, obsessed with the desire to get all of California's beavers, hired anyone he could find, including individuals who had malaria.[6] Of all the groups he sent south, the one that appears to have been most instrumental in spreading malaria to the natives of California was a group led by a trapper named John Work in 1833. As that group went south, it spread malaria through the native people all the way from the Columbia to the southern end of the San Joaquin Valley.[7] When his group was traveling south through the Central Valley, he recorded in his journal that native villages along the rivers were full of people but, later

---

5. Later, when ranches began filling the San Joaquin Valley, hogs were herded into tule areas to eat the roots (Mayfield 1929:122). This further complicated the ecology of streams and marshes.

6. Cook 1956.

7. Cook 1978:92.

that year, when they were returning north, the same villages were empty and littered with bodies and skeletons.

The disease spread very rapidly among native people because the *Anopheles* mosquito, which carries the parasite from person to person, is indigenous to Oregon and California and very abundant along mosquito-rich rivers in both states. Early settlers complained of swarms of mosquitoes so dense that you could not see through them.[8] Consequently, native people near rivers and marshes began dying very rapidly. People who were not yet infected began carrying for those infected, but soon abandoned the sick and dying and fled in terror. Some may have escaped by going up into the higher foothills of the Sierra Nevada; an altitude as little as 400 feet was enough to avoid most of the mosquitoes. Among the Nisenan Maidu living near the Sacramento River, there was a tribal chief who died while many of his offspring, wisely sent to villages higher in the Sierras, survived.

Fatalities along the San Joaquin River were great, in part because the sloughs and the numbers of mosquitoes they generated were enlarged as the beaver dams upstream disintegrated.[9] Many of the Chowchilla died, but, since about one-third of the Chowchilla homeland had an elevation greater than 400 feet, the number of fatalities was probably lower than that of the Nupchenchi at the river. Cook compiled and analyzed a large amount of data concerning the epidemic and came to the stunning conclusion that approximately 75 percent of the native population died from malaria at that time.[10]

Other epidemics spread through the San Joaquin Valley after that. Smallpox ravaged the native population in 1837 and 1844. The first of these two epidemics was caused by Russian trappers arriving at Fort Ross in Sonoma County north of San Francisco. Unfortunately, it spread down the middle of the state and hit the missions nearest to the Chowchilla, killing half of the native people who had remained there after secularization. The smallpox was then transmitted to the Chowchilla, where, according to Cook, the population was decimated.[11] The second epidemic was caused when an American immigrant family brought the disease from the east and settled in Stockton. From there, the disease was transmitted to the Yokuts, including the Chowchilla.[12]

---

8. Davis 1967:15.
9. Cook 1976a:213, 274.
10. Cook 1955:322.
11. Cook 1939:184–187.
12. Cook 1976a:214; Gray 1993:138–139.

These times of disease were terrible years for the Chowchilla. Cremation fires seemed to be constantly burning and all of the native people were weighed down by the misery and sorrow of losing loved friends and relatives. Women burned off their hair, smeared pitch, charcoal, and dirt on themselves, and wailed through the night.[13] All of the survivors felt the excruciating anguish of being left behind, not able to comprehend who was killing them or why. The final tally of the deaths from all of the epidemics from 1833 to 1848 was horrific. Cook estimated that disease killed five times as many natives as were killed by warfare or homicide in the years before the Gold Rush,[14] and that more than 60 percent of the native people had died from introduced diseases alone by that time. This is all we know about the effect of the epidemics on the Chowchilla, but if 60 percent of the Chowchillas had died by 1848, there would be only about 400 of them remaining when the Gold Rush began.

13. Spier 1978:480; Mayfield [1929] 1997:91; Collins 1949:82; Phillips 1997:152.
14. Cook 1976a:215–216; 1955:56–70.

5

Yokuts Resistance and
the Arrival of James Savage

By 1828, all of the northern Yokuts—the Chowchilla, Chukchansi, Siakumne, Tawalumne, Lakisamne, etc.—had horses and were excellent riders. They had also abandoned the flatlands near the San Joaquin River and moved into the Sierra foothills as a matter of defense. The Mexicans were forced by their own system to go farther and farther into the foothills to find new "converts." What they discovered, however, was that these tribes were no longer peaceful people in scattered villages that could be easily taken. They had gathered around new leaders and consolidated into larger villages at defensible sites. Many of the new leaders were former mission captives who had escaped, like Jose Rey and Jose Juarez,[1] and they brought back knowledge of the soldiers' tactics and weaknesses. They also brought guns, although very little ammunition.

One of the first great Yokuts leaders to fight the Mexicans who had inherited the mission system was Estanislao, the Lakisamne Yokuts for whom the Stanislaus River was named. While incarcerated at Mission San Jose in the 1820s, he had witnessed the hardships and brutality that Yokuts endured at the hands of the Mexicans. At the same time, he was positioned as a leader of the natives at the mission and had been given the role of *alcalde* (overseer) by the priests. This gave him greater insight into the mission system and also gave him the privilege of visiting relatives in his homeland without military escort. Taking advantage of this, he led 400 Yokuts back to the Sierra foothills in 1827. These men formed the beginning of an army and, for a year, Estanislao recruited additional

---

1. Phillips 1993:98.

men to that group to fight the Mexican forces.[2] Amazingly, by the end of that year, he had increased his army tenfold. Some of the 4,000 warriors were from Yokuts tribes farther south, while others were from Miwok and more distant tribes. Warriors of the Chumash tribe, for example, who had participated in the revolts at Mission Santa Inéz, Mission Santa Barbara, and Mission La Purisima, heard of Estanislao's leadership and walked en masse from the southern coast to join him.[3]

After many raids upon Mexican farms and towns, Estanislao and his men moved to the protection of two forts on the Stanislaus River built with the help of a group of American trappers led by Ewing Young.[4] Fighting from the daunting palisaded fortifications of these forts, Estanislao could safely send out his warriors to strike at missions with guerrilla tactics. In retaliation, the Mexicans attacked the fortifications three times with cannon and firearms, and the natives, armed mainly with bows and arrows, soundly defeated them twice. In the third attack, the Mexicans could not conquer the larger fort so they set the forest on fire. While this destroyed the fort, it also caused the Mexicans' own defeat because the fire allowed Estanislao and his followers to slip out of the fortress undetected and disappear into the higher foothills.[5]

The battles, however, changed Estanislao. Many Yokuts had been killed by Mexican guns and he blamed himself for their deaths. This cooled his ardor because he knew that the Mexicans would continue to send men until they had killed all of his men. When malaria caused the deaths of many of his men in 1833, Estanislao's spirit was broken and he returned to Mission San Jose to ask for forgiveness from the priests. There, surprisingly, he was protected by Father Duran and subsequently pardoned by the Mexican authorities. He lived there for five years, teaching Mexicans the Yokuts language, before dying in the 1838 smallpox epidemic.[6] Despite this apparent capitulation, Estanislao demonstrated to the Yokuts that natives could outthink and win battles against the better-armed invaders. Justifiably, he has been honored and ranked with such valiant native leaders as Geronimo, Tecumseh, Pontiac, and King Philip.[7]

---

2. Jackson and Castillo 1995:79.
3. Gray 1993:44–45.
4. Gray 1993:44.
5. Gray 1993:44–63.
6. Gray 1993:84.
7. Cook 1962:165.

In the late 1830s, another Lakisamne, named Yoscolo,[8] emerged to take Estanislao's place. Yoscolo brought a different, more aggressive approach to Yokuts resistance. Whereas Estanislao stressed raiding without loss of life, Yoscolo violently raided the missions and ranchos. Ranch buildings were burned and individual Mexican officers who had led barbaric assaults on the native villages were singled out and killed.[9] His army swept into the district of Monterey, which the Mexicans thought would never be invaded. These attacks, of course, alarmed the Mexican population, and soldiers were sent out to find and execute Yoscolo. When this ploy did not succeed, the Mexican government put a price on Yoscolo's head and circulated an offer of reward among native men who, they thought, would have better luck finding him. However, Yoscolo was always surrounded by armed warriors and unreachable by a would-be assassin. Raids upon Mexican ranches and towns continued for a year and a half after the Monterey raid. Then, in 1838, the Mexican forces came up with a new strategy. They selected a large native man and trained him in hand-to-hand combat. This man could easily walk into a native village and, using a Yokuts tradition of settling wars with a duel of champions, could challenge Yoscolo to a duel. The plan worked, and Yoscolo was overmatched and killed in the duel.[10]

Estanislao and Yoscolo were important because they demonstrated military leadership and introduced military tactics not previously known to the Yokuts. However, some of the Yokuts tribes were not ready to unite and follow the two leaders at the beginning and the end of the 1830s. The reluctant Yokuts tribes, like the Choinumne, believed that fighting was futile and the best approach was to maintain their traditional, peaceful way of life. Others, like the Chowchilla, saw that strength lay in the unity of the warriors of their tribe rather than in unity with other tribes. The time was coming, however, when the Chowchilla would stand and greet other Yokuts and Miwoks as brothers in the same fight. That time would come, as we will see in the next chapter, when gold was discovered and American miners began to come onto their land in great numbers.

In the intervening years, between the final missions' secularization and the acquisition of California by the United States in 1848, the state was composed of about 450 large, independent ranchos, many with land grants, and several small but growing pueblos. Each rancho had its own

8. Yoscolo wore a mask when he was fighting and is said to have been the origin of the Zorro myth.
9. Gray 1993:83–84.
10. Gray 1993:86.

army, composed of former presidio soldiers and local ruffians, to fend off and punish native attacks. This meant that military power was fragmented, uncoordinated, and uncontrolled. And, as we saw in the previous chapter, the soldiers of the armies had complete license to deal with native people as they pleased.

The war that the Chowchilla fought in those years was, in consequence, a hit-and-run, guerrilla war, employing the night raid method previously developed. The most significant change in their raids was the use of scouts to determine which rancho was most vulnerable and which had the most horses and mules. With the collapse of the missions, native people were, in theory, released to return to the homelands, but in reality many of the released Yokuts were captured once again and found themselves as virtual slaves on the ranchos. The only thing good about this was that they could pass information to the scouts, not only about the livestock at the rancho, but about when and where the rancho men would be attacking villages in the foothills. These poor people imprisoned at the ranchos had little or no hope of ever seeing their homeland again, but by helping the scouts they could assist in the flow of horses and mules to their relatives in the villages. The reports of Mexican attacks compiled by Cook (1962) reveal that there was a steady flow of this livestock to the native villages, and that the Mexicans were notorious for their inability to recover any the livestock taken from the ranchos. This is testament to the fighting talents of the Chowchilla, of course, but also to the help from the people at the ranchos.

Another aspect of the conflict in the decade before the Gold Rush was the increase in the enslavement of native people. This obscene practice had existed from the beginning of the Spanish years, but it was more common in the early 1840s, primarily because rancheros competed for slaves, which this drove the price of a slave up. There were gangs of men, independent of the ranchos, who made a living by seizing native people while slaughtering everyone who challenged them.[11] Most of these gangs were made up of immoral and cruel white men, but there were also gangs of native men from one tribe who kidnapped members of a traditional enemy tribe to sell to the ranchos.[12] Captured natives were herded on a grueling march to the rancho, where they would be divided by their sex and age, bought and sold, traded, and even rented out to other ranchos. John Sutter, who had established himself in the Central Valley in 1839, adopted the custom of slavery

---

11. Hurtado 2006:209.
12. Hurtado 2006:74.

as practiced by the Mexican rancheros, and even described it in his correspondence. In 1843, he was on the verge of losing his lands, fort and all, because he had a bad harvest and had foolishly accumulated a huge debt. He turned to native slavery to pay his debts. He was hired by rancheros to punish Yokuts villages, where some were horse thieves, but his wages for doing that were small compared to the money he got for selling the Yokuts people as slaves to ranchos throughout the state.[13]

In contrast to Sutter and the other slave drivers, there were a growing number of American settlers in the Central Valley who were farming families, and who treated native people in a humane way. These families were generally isolated from towns, ranchos, and other farmer families, and it was thus a matter of self-interest and survival that they treated native people with respect. Their existence depended upon peaceful coexistence. At the same time, they had to exist in the midst of violence against the native people emanating from the ranchos, and it was not in their self-interest for them to make their friendship with native people widely known. For this reason, there are few records that describe their relationships with the local native people. Two exceptions are the Mayfield family living with the Choinumne Yokuts, and the Bidwell family living with the Konkow Maidu.[14]

There are considerably more records that show the reverse situation, namely, native leaders and people seeking peaceful coexistence with white people. These cases are frequently in the context of extreme animosity from the white people that they wished to befriend. In those cases, they, too, were acting for self-preservation. If you have read *Indian Summer*, describing the peaceful Mayfield-Choinumne relationship, you will be shocked to know that it happened just after the chief of that tribe and all of the native people in his village were massacred by American white men. I will tell more about this massacre later in this book, because it triggered an important change in the fate of the Chowchilla.

It is impossible to understand the actions of the native people in the foothills of the Sierras in this time frame unless one brings to mind what should be obvious, namely, that virtually all behavior became based upon self-preservation. Some Nisenan, Miwok, and Yokuts chiefs, for example, started to recruit people from their tribes to leave their homes and work

---

13. Hurtado has ably chronicled Sutter's slave trade in Sutter's correspondence (2006:39, 50, 154). The Yokuts tribes who were the targets of Sutter's inhumanity are not known.
14. Mayfield [1929] 1997; Bidwell 1890.

at ranchos that were considered friendly. Some chiefs not only ceased raiding, but joined forces with men from particular ranchos in pursuing and punishing raiders from other tribes.

One of these chiefs was Jose Jesus, the chief of the Siakumne Yokuts, whose homeland was about 60 miles north of the Chowchilla homeland on the Stanislaus River. Jose Jesus had been captured and taken to Mission Santa Clara, but, when he returned in 1839, he resumed his role as the chief and quickly extended his domination on the east side of the San Joaquin River from the Mokelumne River in the north to the Tuolumne River in the south. This gave him control over approximately 1,000 people and made it possible for him to form sizable groups of warriors.[15] When this became known, the rancheros in the Valley braced for attacks. Rumors circulated that he was the successor to Estanislao and Yoscolo and that big battles were in store. However, the big battles never occurred. Jose Jesus was torn between the Mexican lifestyle, which he admired, and the Mexican priests and soldiers, whom he hated. He carried great resentment and anger toward the Mexicans as the result of the tortures and deprivations that he saw and experienced in the mission, and he constantly sought opportunities to fight Mexicans, but he always dressed like a Mexican, wearing a sash, serape, and sombrero.

Jose Jesus saw no reason to defend traditional native cultures, and when American trade goods became available, he actively promoted their use in his villages. Perhaps because of this, he was a faithful ally of John Sutter and American settlers for the rest of his life. He provided a steady flow of native labor to help Sutter and the settlers in harvesting and herding. He brought warriors to join Sutter's military force and led expeditions to punish native villages that were stealing livestock from the ranches and settlements. In 1846, when the United States went to war against Mexico, John Fremont tried unsuccessfully to recruit American settlers around Sacramento to march against the Mexicans at Los Angeles. The American men declined to volunteer because, they said, native people would destroy their farms if they left. Sutter sent word to Jose Jesus about the new army and the chief immediately appeared with 18 Yokuts warriors and joined the force, later called the California Battalion, which was instrumental in making California an American state.[16] After that, Jose Jesus sent some

---

15. Phillips 1993:97, 130.
16. Hurtado 1988:81–82.

of his people to work in American gold mining camps,[17] and, when the United States sent commissioners to make peace treaties with the tribes of California in 1851, he served as a representative of his people. Ironically, he was on his way to sign the peace treaty when a white man who thought he looked dangerous shot and killed him.[18]

The Chowchilla, on the other hand, resented the aggressive Americans as well as the Mexicans. Nevertheless, Jose Jesus's involvement in the California Battalion turned out to be a significant event for the Chowchilla, because it was on the long ride to Los Angeles and back that Jose Jesus met and befriended a muscular, blond American named James Savage, who would play a critical role in the survival of the Chowchilla. Several Yokuts tribes would be totally annihilated and would vanish as Americans swept through California. James Savage, as we will see, was the unlikely hero that prevented this from happening to the Chowchilla.

Savage had come to California on a wagon train from Illinois, arriving at Sutter's Fort on October 28, 1846, just before the hostilities between the Americans and the Mexicans referred to above began. He had lost his wife, Eliza, and an unnamed baby daughter to an unknown illness during the trip, and this left him morally unencumbered to join the rough group of men living at Sutter's Fort. At this stage in Savage's life, he was an immoral, untrustworthy bully and thief. Savage stole anything he wanted from anyone he saw, including defenseless women and old people. He drank to excess if liquor was available and picked fights with everyone in camp.[19] However, he had two important, redeeming features: He was empathetic toward native people and learned languages easily. When he was 16, his family moved to Princeton, Illinois, where the Sauk-Fox War with the United States had just ended with the virtual annihilation of a Sauk fighting force led by a chief named Black Hawk. As Savage learned the combatants' languages, he learned that the two tribes had been cheated out of their land by the U.S. government and became convinced that the fight to reclaim the land was a justified and honorable war, even though his family benefited from the war's outcome.[20] He particularly admired Black Hawk, despite the fact that Black Hawk had caused the deaths of 77 Americans and about 550 native warriors who had fought the Americans with him. At the same time, Savage admired another Sauk leader, named Keokuk, who had saved many

17. Phillips 1993:142.
18. Phillips 1997:207.
19. Lienhard [1898] 1941: 18–19, 23; Hurtado 1988:114.
20. Savage's family was enabled to have a farm by the expulsion of the Sauk tribe.

of the Sauk people from the war. Keokuk had visited American cities on the east coast and had become convinced that the Sauk people could not win a war against the large number of Americans that he saw in the cities. For this reason, Keokuk took a large number of Sauk people to safety on the other side of the Mississippi River and away from the war. When Savage got to California 13 years later, the admiration of these two native leaders caused him to relate to the California's native people in a much different manner than his comrades at Sutter's Fort.

During the trip of the California Battalion from Sutter's Fort to Los Angeles to fight the Mexicans, Savage learned that Americans were also mistreating Jose Jesus's tribe and the other Yokuts tribes. Jose Jesus's warriors, for example, were made to camp between the white volunteers and the Mexican forces, so that, if the Mexicans attacked, the native warriors would be the first killed.[21] Nevertheless, Jose Jesus made friends with the Americans in the Battalion, particularly with Savage, who was learning both the Yokuts and Miwok languages. After the Mexicans capitulated and the Battalion was mustered out in April 1847, Jose Jesus invited six Americans, including Savage, to come to Chaspaiseme, his village on the Stanislao River.[22] For Savage, this was an opportunity to learn more of the Yokuts' language and to experience the Yokuts' way of life firsthand.

Savage, however, had bigger plans for this visit. He had been searching for an occupation, a way to support himself. He had experienced farming in Illinois, but such a life did not attract him. In the short time that he was at the fort, before the Battalion and after, he admired Sutter's success in creating an empire with the labor of native people. And then, with Jose Jesus's people, he began to envision a life like Sutter's for himself. It seemed to him an easy thing to do; the native people already treated him as a dignitary simply because he was a white man who spoke their language. But he wanted more status and power than that gave him. Savage decided to convince them that he was possessed superhuman strength. They were, he thought, a simple, superstitious people who could be convinced that he was superhuman by demonstrating his physical strength or by using some trickery. With this in mind, he visited villages north of the Chowchillas. In some he entered into contests of strength with a village champion and in others he used a deceiving stunt. One biographer states that Savage used gunpowder explosions to make a dramatic entrance into a village and used

---

21. Hurtado 2006:201, 203.
22. Now called the Stanislaus River.

a battery to give them electric shocks.[23] Latta interviewed Yokuts people in 1928 who remembered that Savage fired his gun at a tree to show the damage it could do and then, reloading the gun with blanks, asked one of the native men to shoot him.[24]

By the end of the month, he had done much to establish a high status among the Yokuts. He had inveigled the chiefs of five villages to each give him a wife and he had persuaded the villagers to call him *El Rey Güero* (The Blond King).[25] By doing this, Savage proclaimed himself to be the chief of all of the chiefs. However, Savage knew that, to sustain such status, he had to prove that he could provide things that his followers needed or wanted. To do this, he brought trade goods from Sutter's Fort and bestowed these on Yokuts who supported him. Earlier that year (1847), the American Governor of California had issued an edict that native people could not travel individually without passports and could not "go about in crowds." The governor also ordained that regular patrols would enforce these rules. Thus, the Yokuts could not go to the fort's store, but Savage could go for them. Savage left the Yokuts villages in late May and returned to the fort where Sutter was eager to hire him. From Sutter's diary, we know that Savage worked for Sutter for a month and a half until July 12, 1847.[26] During this time, Savage took charge of a group of Sutter's native workers cutting down pine trees near Coloma and bringing wagon loads of lumber to the fort. Sutter's lumber mill at Coloma was not yet finished; for Sutter, Savage's crew was an important source of building material. By the end of that time, he had accumulated considerable wages to purchase trade goods for the Yokuts.

On July 12, Sutter instructed Savage to take "tools, provisions, etc." to another of Sutter's work groups in the mountains,[27] but, strangely, Sutter does not record his return and Savage is not mentioned in the diary for a month. On August 13, 1847, Sutter noted that he arrived from Deer Creek. Three weeks later, Savage again leaves Sutter's employment, but at that time he boarded Sutter's regular boat to the Bay Area. He returned two weeks

23. Traywick, *Big Jim Savage, Blonde King of the Indians*, chapter 4.
24. Cossley-Batt 1928:110; Latta 1949:219.
25. Mitchell 1949:342.
26. Sutter's diary is particularly helpful in tracing Savage's movements. Sutter was constantly looking for nonnative employees with talent. Savage was important to him because he was strong and could communicate with the natives working with him. In addition, Savage stood out in any crowd by being blond; his arrivals and departures were easily observed.
27. Sutter 1939:58.

later on September 23, but, after doing an urgent job for Sutter,[28] he disappears from the diary until February 29, 1848, a month after the discovery of gold, when he arrived with a man named Williams. The two of them stayed one night at the fort and then hurried on to San Jose aboard Sutter's launch.

---

28. John Fremont's men had stolen 150 cattle and Sutter wanted to someone to take a gang of native herders to recover them quickly before native raiders could take them.

6

The Gold Rush and
the Mariposa War

For the native people living near the middle of the mother lode, the Gold Rush was a holocaust. White men had, of course, been among them for many years, but when the Gold Rush started it was as if a dam had broken. Hordes of white men poured onto their land, occupying every streambed with total disregard of the native people. These men were not farmers or ranchers, priests or soldiers; they were miners who spent all of their time scooping up the sediments of streams and rivers or breaking gold-bearing rock. They worked all day long to find gold before other miners could. Nothing else mattered to them. Laws, leadership, social ties, cooperation, families, religion, and all of the other characteristics of human society were irrelevant. Their greed caused them to abandon any moral code that they had ever known while asserting that the native people were the ones who were amoral and, hence, dangerous heathens. If the native people fought back or just got in the way, the white men insisted that they, the invaders, were innocent victims and that the native people should be punished for breaking "laws" that the whites themselves had devised, even if the laws were patently immoral and/or illogical. As mentioned above, the state government made a law that prohibited native people from going out together to the hills to collect and transport the enormous amounts of acorns they depended on, or to gather at the rivers to catch and smoke the tons of salmon that they needed to sustain themselves for most of the year. Exposed to this sort of rule, as well as to the introduced diseases and mindless violence, the tribes of native people in the center of the mother lode area were decimated. Their cultures were destroyed so rapidly that who and what they were may never be accurately known.

Fortunately, this does not accurately describe what happened at the edges of the mother lode. The Chowchilla and other tribes at the southern end of the mother lode, for example, were able to maintain their tribal unity and to resist the invasion of the miners, perhaps because the number of miners was small or because the natives had experienced the invasions of Spaniards and Mexicans and had learned that it was very unlikely that native people would be treated fairly by *any* white man. Nevertheless, the native people were anxious to obtain the trade goods possessed by the white men, and it was easy for the white miners to get native people to collect gold for them.

To a great extent, James Savage brought the Gold Rush to the Chowchillas. As I noted in the last chapter, he had previously established trading posts for Yokuts farther north as a direct outcome of the Americans' rules prohibiting any movement by individuals and groups of native people. In those trading posts, he was giving the native people trade goods in exchange for his "royal" status and the cooperation of the Yokuts. When gold was discovered, he shifted to exchanging trade goods for gold and, simultaneously, moved south, away from his principal tribal supporters. In effect, he gave up his crown when he started to enter into partnerships with other white men to mine for gold. He did not cut all of his ties with the Yokuts people; he was counting on them to bring the gold to his trading posts. But relationships with the tribes deteriorated and eventually became reduced to communication with them through his five wives.

Savage's first move toward the south was in November 1848, when he joined three other white men in a mining venture at the headwaters of the Tuolumne River near Jamestown. Early in 1849, he and his partners moved 15 miles down the Tuolumne in search of richer deposits. These two camps were near the border between Miwok and Yokuts tribes, but, despite the fact that they messed up the streams, there were no physical conflicts between Savage's group and the native people in these two camps. In the fall of 1849, Savage gave up the hard work of mining, left the partnership, and established a trading post 20 miles farther south on the Merced River. This, however, turned out to be a mistake because, without knowing it, he located his post well within Miwok territory, 15 miles from Yosemite Valley. Soon after he arrived, warriors of a Miwok tribe from Yosemite Valley attacked his post.[1] Savage and his men repulsed the attack,

---

1. Although commonly referred to as Miwok, this tribe was actually a mixture of Miwok people and belligerent Shoshone (Paiute) people from the other side of the Sierras.

but he decided to pull up stakes and move again in early 1850. This time his move was a double move. He first went to Agua Fria, where quartz veins containing gold had been discovered. Many miners were attracted by this discovery and the place quickly became a ragtag camp of men willing to tackle the daunting task of breaking rock that might contain gold. The large number of miners meant two things to Savage: First, there were too many white men with guns for the native warriors to attack, and, second, the wares of a trading post would be in demand. However, the place also had drawbacks. It was higher in the Sierras, in rugged territory. The dangers posed by the Miwok were amplified by the dangers of lawless miners, and maintaining a well-stocked trading post with goods from the Bay Area or Monterey would be difficult. More important, Savage knew or quickly discovered that exploiting the labor of the native people was much easier than bargaining with unruly miners, and mining hard rock deposits called for many fewer native workers than mining placers. Savage consequently also established a trading post in the foothills where the placer deposits had been formed by long weathering of the Agua Fria rock. The place he chose was on the Fresno River at a point that could be forded by wagons in the rainy season, a place that came to be called Fresno Crossing. In addition, the trading post would be on the boundary between the Chowchilla Tribe to the west and the Chukchansi Tribe to the east. There would be many natives who could be enticed to bring gold to the post.

The placer deposits below Fresno Crossing were in sediments of the Mariposa, Chowchilla, Fresno, and San Joaquin Rivers. The first three of these rivers were in the territory of the Chowchilla, who were well known for their livestock raids on ranches and farms. Savage, however, seems to have befriended their chiefs with gifts and whetted their appetites for trade goods in exchange for gold. However, he soon found himself surrounded by natives from multiple Yokuts tribes who were interested in his merchandise. The San Joaquin River, only 15 miles south of the Chowchilla, marked the southern end of the mother lode. There were no significant placers farther south, and Yokuts tribes from that area had no access to trade goods unless they came north and competed with the Chowchilla and Chukchansi.

The collection of gold from the placers by all of these native people was rapid, and Savage soon had an immense amount of gold. The competition among the natives was great, and he had no scruples against raising his prices to extreme levels. A pound of novel foods, like sugar and raisins,

Figure 8. The Fresno River near the location of James Savage's trading post

would cost a pound of gold. Blankets and cloth were worth more than their weight in gold.[2] By November 1850, Savage had kegs of gold in his tent worth many thousands of dollars. However, while Savage reveled in his riches, animosity was rising among the native people. White miners continued to arrive throughout the foothills north of the San Joaquin, and the Chowchilla in particular saw the danger of their usurpation. There were rumors, conveyed to Savage by his wives, that the Chowchilla would soon attack the post on the Fresno River. This prompted Savage to take $50,000 worth of gold to San Francisco and to take one of the Chowchilla

---

2. Brownlee 1986:127; Harris 1960:146.

chiefs, Jose Juarez, with him. Remembering the effect on Keokuk of seeing big east coast cities. Savage thought that, if Jose Juarez saw how many white people there were in San Francisco, the chief would see that war with the whites would be an act of tribal suicide.

What happened in San Francisco is not entirely known. Savage told Brunnell that Jose Juarez became so obnoxiously drunk and verbally abusive that Savage had to restrain him physically.[3] However, another white man, William Howard, who had close contacts among the Yokuts, stated that while drinking in a tavern, Savage recklessly wagered all or most of the gold on a single bet and lost. Since Savage had promised to use the gold to buy blankets for the Chowchilla, Jose Juarez became angry and castigated him in front of a group of laughing men for losing the gold. Savage, angered by this public criticism, knocked Jose Juarez down with one punch.[4] Regardless of what actually happened, this punch made it impossible for Jose Juarez to emulate Keokuk. When they returned to the Fresno post, Jose Juarez rose before an assembled group of Chowchilla and other Yokuts and Miwok leaders and encouraged them to wage war on the whites. The city dwellers, he said, were from many different tribes, and would not come to the aid of the miners. When he was finished speaking, Jose Rey, the highest-ranking chief of the Chowchilla tribe,[5] rose and solemnly walked to the center of the circle of native leaders, followed by two important Pitkachi Yokuts chiefs, Tomquit and Frederico. When all eyes were on him, he said, "My people are now ready to wage war against the white gold miners."[6]

Two weeks later, on December 17, 1850, the Miwok natives around the Agua Fria post abruptly left for the mountains as a group. Savage, thinking that the Miwoks might be massing to attack in numbers, went after them with 16 men and caught up with them more than 30 miles into the Sierras, when the Miwoks were on the opposite side of a gorge. The leader of this retreating group was Bautista, a Miwok chief whose father had been

---

3. Bunnell 1880:4.
4. Bunnell 1880:4–5; Cossley-Batt 1928:112.
5. From later incidents, it seems likely that Jose Rey was the Eagle Moiety Chief of the Chowchilla and Jose Juarez was the Coyote Moiety Chief. After this confrontation, Jose Juarez is not mentioned in the descriptions of confrontations and may have been killed in an early battle of the Mariposa War.
6. Phillips 1997:43–44.

executed without cause by an angry American army officer.[7] Yelling across the gorge, Bautista acknowledged that he was taking the Miwok women and children to a safe place in preparation for a war with the whites. He boasted to Savage that the tribes were united and that they would push the white intruders out of their land. Bautista then revealed that, while Savage was absent from the Fresno trading post, it had been destroyed and all of Savage's men killed. Savage immediately rushed to Fresno Crossing to find that Bautista had been telling the truth; the post had been plundered by Chowchilla warriors and three of his four men had been brutally killed.

To the miners, this was the first battle of a war, but, to the Chowchilla, it was a necessary step to show the invaders that they could and would defend their Yokuts territory from invasion. The Chowchilla leaders, Jose Rey and Jose Juarez, now wore the mantle of multitribal leadership once worn by Estanislao and Yoscolo, and, in the next few weeks, they drew together warriors from four Yokuts tribes and three Miwok tribes.[8] Subsequently, in several parts of the Mariposa area, miners were driven out. Near the Merced River, Rattlesnake Creek, and Bear Valley, white settlements were attacked and miners forced to leave.[9] Farther south, on the San Joaquin, the mining operation at Cassady's Bar was attacked and the miners driven out.[10] Alsbury's ferry on the Merced, which provided access to the southern mines, was attacked and the station stripped of its horses and cattle.[11]

These scattered, unpredictable attacks caused great alarm among the miners. A spontaneous vigilante group of 74 men was formed and, without adequate supplies or ammunition, they rushed up the Chowchilla River to "punish" the natives. Late on January 10, 1851, with Savage guiding them, they sighted a village on a hillside and the next day at daybreak the group attacked. As they approached, a dog in the village started barking and the natives in the village rapidly disappeared into the underbrush. Seeing this and thinking that the natives were giving up without a fight, the vigilantes immediately charged the village. The ensuing fight was completely disorga-

---

7. Crampton 1957:20. In 1847, an arrogant American officer, Henry Naglee, accused Bautista's father, a Miwok chief, of stealing horses. When the chief denied this, Naglee angrily summoned a firing squad and, when the chief again denied stealing horses, he executed the chief and a companion on the spot. Bautista's dying father made Bautista promise that he would avenge his death. Much later Bautista befriended the Americans (cf. *Sam Ward in the Gold Rush*, C. Collins, ed.).

8. Bunnell 1880:12–13.

9. Letter from Burney to the governor, Jan. 13, 1851.

10. Bunnell 1880:10.

11. Phillips 1997:47.

nized. Vigilantes ran in every direction, shooting wherever they thought the natives might be hiding. When a cease-fire was called a few minutes later, they discovered that they had killed one of their own leaders and seriously wounded three other vigilantes. They discovered that the village consisted of only two houses with three natives, two boys and an old woman. The boys had been killed in the wild firing and the woman had been wounded. All of the other natives were hidden in the underbrush firing arrows at the vigilantes in the open village area. The vigilantes, finding themselves now surrounded, were forced to retreat in defeat.[12]

Savage waited for reinforcements and supplies for a few days while dealing with the wounded. When the number of vigilantes reached 100, Savage led them out to follow the natives who the vigilantes believed were running away in fear. After a week of tracking, they found a large village on a rugged mountaintop containing about 500 native people. This was a confederation of tribes that had joined for the fight. The village included Chowchilla, Chukchansi, Nootchu, Potoyante, Pohonochee, Kaweah, and Yosemite warriors under the Chowchilla leadership of Jose Rey. The next morning Savage's party attacked the village with a wild charge, setting fire to the houses. The village people, forewarned again, went into the underbrush where they could fire arrows into the vigilantes without being seen. Some of the warriors, following tradition, came out of hiding and challenged Savage to fight one-on-one, only to be killed in a volley of rifle fire.[13] As the skirmish continued, the fire the vigilantes had set began to spread down the mountain, threatening their own supplies. The vigilantes then had to retreat to save their camp. Arguing that they had won the fight, the vigilantes then turned back to Agua Fria. Some of the vigilantes had been wounded but none died. Twenty-three native bodies were counted, but more were wounded and may have died.[14] More important, the great Chowchilla chief, Jose Rey, had been badly wounded.[15]

When the vigilantes reached Agua Fria, they sent a report about the fight to the governor, exaggerating both how successful they had been and how dangerous the native warriors were. They reported that the native fighters had caused the bullet wounds of their men and the death of the vigilante

---

12. Cossley-Batt 1928:123–125.
13. Crampton 1957:23.
14. Savage estimated 40–50 natives were killed.
15. Bunnell 1880:14. Different reports of these two battles contradict each other. Here the battles are described on the basis of mutually compatible data in Bunnell (1880), Clampton (1957), and Cossley-Batt (1928).

leader in the earlier fighting.[16] This inflammatory letter asked for government assistance, but it was unnecessary. Before it arrived at the capital, the governor had already taken action on the basis of other, equally unreliable reports, authorizing a unit of the state's volunteer militia to fight the native group. Since this meant getting paid for fighting, the unit soon had 200 men for what was called the Mariposa Battalion.[17]

After his vigilante experiences, Savage realized that the success of the battalion hinged upon discipline and organization. Given the rank of major, he took the volunteers into camp to train them. However, before Savage could finish preparing them for action, he received new orders from the governor. He was to suspend military action until three federal commissioners, George Barbour, O. M. Wozencraft, and Redick McKee arrived. These commissioners had been sent by the federal government to make peace treaties with all of the tribes of California and the state governor sent word that the battalion was to assist in achieving this goal. The battalion consequently waited for the commissioners while the native warriors continued their pressure on the whites, disrupting mining activity and stealing horses and mules—including some of the battalion's horse herd.[18] When the commissioners finally arrived, new orders were in store for the battalion. The battalion was to be controlled by the commissioners. It was to shed its image as a pack of vigilantes and to act as representatives of the federal government, not the state of California or the local population. Further, they could act only when tribes refused to cease their attacks and make treaties.[19]

The new commissioners restrained the battalion and sent runners to inform the tribes of their arrival and purpose. Within a few days, small parties of Miwoks and Yokuts began arriving at the commissioners' camp on the Fresno. These early arrivals were rewarded with feasts and gifts, and soon more chiefs began arriving to indicate their willingness to negotiate. Significantly, among the tribes that came in was Bautista's tribe, the

---

16. Cossley-Batt 1928:130–132; 136–137. William Howard, who spoke Yokuts and served on the initial forays as well as in the battalion, was of the opinion that many of the difficulties in white-native conflict stemmed from James Savage's megalomania. When Savage first arrived among the Yokuts, he wanted to be called *El Rey Güero* (the blond king) or *El Rey Tulareños* (the king of the Yokuts).

17. Bunnell 1880:15.

18. Bunnell 1880:39.

19. Bunnell 1880:39–40.

Potoyante. When Bautista signed the treaty on March 19, 1851, his tribe was the first to abandon the confederation that fought under Jose Rey.

After this first treaty, the battalion was sent out to bring in other tribes by threatening them with annihilation. The Pohonochi Miwoks and Nootchu Yokuts quickly capitulated to Savage's threats. A few days later, the Yosemite Miwoks,[20] under the great chief, Tenaya, yielded and began marching to the commissioners' camp with guards from Savage's battalion. As this guarded group of natives neared the camp, Savage left the battalion to precede them into the commissioners' camp. The remaining Americans, under the command of John Bowling, let down their guard and allowed Chowchilla runners to sneak in at night and convince the Yosemite Miwoks to flee.[21] Savage quickly went after them and, after a few more dire threats, Tenaya's Miwoks joined the others at the treaty camp. At that point, of the original confederation of tribes, only the Chowchilla and Chukchansi remained hostile.

The Chowchilla fought on, attacking mining camps and taking horses. Recognizing the seductiveness of the Americans' gifts, they attempted to undermine the treaty process by visiting the villages of different tribes and expressing their doubts about the veracity and peaceful intent of the whites. Tribes that had taken part of Jose Rey's confederacy would be separated and killed, they said. If the tribes united and attacked the farms and mining camps, the native people would be able to drive the whites off of their land.

In the meantime, Savage convinced the commissioners that it was necessary to exert military force to get the Chowchilla to come in and make a treaty.[22] He assembled a troop of about 100 men and quickly set out to attack them on April 14, 1851. Shortly after leaving the camp, however, the commissioners called him back to assist in negotiations with his knowledge of native languages. Without Savage, the Chowchilla campaign continued under the leadership of Captain Bowling, who took his men on an arduous march of more than 100 miles into the Sierras and back without finding any Chowchilla. They found empty villages and large caches of acorns, which they destroyed, but no Chowchilla. Their most important discovery was a large empty village with a large pile of ashes. Upon close inspection, they found that the pile of ashes contained the personal belongings of Jose Rey. The great chief had died of his wounds and had been cremated by a large

20. The Yosemite natives were a mixture of local Miwoks and Paiutes from the other side of the Sierras. When Savage's troops approached, the Paiutes fled back over the mountains.
21. Bunnell 1880:96–97.
22. Bunnell 1880:99.

gathering of native people. This was stunning news. However, the news had already reached the commissioners. When Bowling's troops returned, they were greeted with the news that the Chowchilla representatives had been there for several days and had already signed a peace treaty![23]

Prior to Bowling's troops arrival, Tomquit and Frederico, the Pitkachi chiefs who had supported Jose Rey from the beginning, sent a Kaweah Yokuts chief to the commissioners' camp to tell them that the Chowchillas were unable to feed their families, but, fearing the white man's "medicine," they would starve rather than come in. No one knew what to do about this incredible message, but, as the commissioners stood talking, one person understood the message and stepped forward to act: James Savage. He had exploited natives and killed natives, but now a new James Savage emerged. He quickly rounded up a few of steers that had been meant for the soldiers' rations and took them to the Chowchilla.[24] After the steers had been butchered and eaten, Savage convinced them that the white man's "medicine" would help them and they would not be harmed. To everyone's surprise, 17 of the feared Chowchilla walked into the commissioners' camp with Savage.[25] When asked who their leader was, a 16-year-old boy named Poholeel came from the group. The commissioners at first doubted that a boy that young could be the chief of the Chowchilla, but Savage had spoken with them in their own language and he confirmed that Poholeel was the brother of Jose Rey and, hence, the new chief. A few days later, on April 29, 1851, Poholeel and four other Chowchilla (Ekeeno, Kayoya, Apemshee, and Chonohalma) accepted the terms of the treaty and signed it, along with representatives from the Chukchansi and 14 other tribes. Soon after this, Poholeel and the other Chowchilla voluntarily followed Savage to a new reservation on the San Joaquin River a few miles south of Fort Miller.

In retrospect, it is difficult to understand Savage's behavior through this period. He seemed eager to completely abandon his native workers and the gold they gave him for trade goods. It was possible for him to move south of the San Joaquin River, where there were Yokuts tribes that liked Americans and willingly signed their treaties. Instead, he chose to fight those that opposed and hated the Americans. However, there was something that he saw and others had not seen. The gold from the placers was dwindling rapidly. After only three years, there were so many miners looking for it

23. Crampton 1957:79; Phillips 1997:93–94.
24. Bunnell 1880:125.
25. Phillips 1997:93. This was not all of the surviving Chowchilla, but the others came in later.

and so little gold remaining that trading posts began to be abandoned and miners drifted away to other more profitable places. For those that stayed in the area, the Gold Rush became a land rush, as former miners competed for the best farmland. In addition, native people were required to live on reservations, which, for their own safety, they did not wish to leave. It was no longer possible for someone like Savage to send out a large number of native workers to bring in small amounts of gold dust. For the new James Savage, a government paycheck for overseeing a reservation became an attractive opportunity.

7

Treaties and Reservations

During the first two years of the Gold Rush, the violence perpetrated by miners against the native people reached a bloody crescendo everywhere in the mother lode area. The situation was so dire that Peter Burnett, Governor of California, concluded that the violence would not end until the native people became extinct.[1] Eventually, the U.S. Senate decided to intervene and sent the three commissioners to make peace treaties with the tribes, through which reservations would be established to separate and protect the native people. The Senate omitted most of the details concerning how the commissioners would do this, but two unspoken goals were implied in their instructions. One of these was that the native land that white people had found useful must be vacated by the native people and given to white people. The other was that native people must abandon their traditional cultures.

With the help of the military and many gifts, made or promised, for the native people, the commissioners were incredibly successful in producing peace agreements. Eighteen treaties were made with 119 tribes or nations. Each of the treaties identified the boundaries of sizable reservations from the Mexican border to the Oregon border. And all of these treaties were made and sent to Washington for ratification within a single year. However, the rapidity with which the treaties were written by the commissioners made it inevitable that they were based upon incorrect information and unrealizable assumptions. For example, it was assumed that, since the natives already lived in nature under very rough circumstances, they could be moved anywhere. Further, it was assumed that, when the native people became familiar with civilized life, they would welcome new tools and adaptations and would ardently desire to adopt the white way of life.

---

1. Quoted in Hurtado 1988:134–135.

The commissioners also made poor decisions in constructing and managing the treaties. They acknowledged that the native people lived in tribes that had leaders and spoke a common language, but they nevertheless assumed that, if the natives had societies with traditional social structure, laws, and beliefs, these aspects of native life were not worthy of consideration. It did not matter to them which members of a tribe signed the treaties. Indeed, it did not even matter whether the "tribes" or "nations" identified in the treaties were actually tribes. A much later investigation revealed that 59 of the 139 tribes and nations identified in the treaties were actually villages and two others were single individuals. Even when they had the right tribal name, many of the signatories were not chiefs and had no authority to represent the tribe with which they were identified. Some individuals appear to have signed for a tribe other than their own.[2]

These problems merely scratch the surface. In retrospect, it is clear that, if the treaties had become law, the California's native people would have suffered greatly and the cost of straightening out the mess would be many times that of the initial treaties. As it was, voices were immediately raised in the California legislature against the treaties, not because the treaties were flawed but because the treaties were biased toward the native people.[3] A litany of false charges was levied against the commissioners and the treaties. Some of the arguments made against the treaties were (1) the commissioners were said to have given too much land to the native people and the land they gave away included the state's most valuable agricultural and mineral land; (2) the treaties were too expensive; (3) the white residents of California were already protecting and educating the natives; and (4) the natives would soon be extinct so the treaties were meaningless. In fact, the commissioners had designated a mere 7 percent of California as reservations in exchange for all of the rest of the state west of the crest of the Sierras, and they had designated some of the poorest, most out-of-the-way land in the state as adequate for the natives. Much of this land would be difficult for anyone to use, let alone people who had no traditions of wresting a living from the soil.[4] When the natives were moved to the reservations, as many later were, they endured great hardship in adapting

2. Heizer and Almquist 1971:76. The numbers produced by this investigation are somewhat suspect because, as Kroeber pointed out (1925:831), the name of the tribe was not uncommonly the name of the chief's village. Hence, a treaty with a chief's village was a treaty with the tribe. Further, in that case, the tribe's name would or could change if the chief moved to another village (as in the malaria epidemic, for example).

3. Hurtado 1988:140.

4. Phillips 1997:72.

to strange and scarce food sources. Many would attempt to return to their old land, only to find that white residents now claimed the land and water, and violence between whites and natives was renewed. There was, in fact, ample evidence available to the commissioners that the treaties would not have ended violence toward the native people, but, rather, would have hurried them toward extinction.

Back in Washington, the U.S. Senate rejected the treaties on July 8, 1852, for political reasons.[5] Then, to mislead the leaders of the native people into thinking that they were now at peace with and friends of the whites, the senators concealed the rejection of the treaties in secret files that were not opened until 1905, fifty-four years later. Nevertheless, government agents in California began moving the native people to reservations in the Central Valley as soon as the treaties were signed.

The treaty that committed the Chowchilla and fifteen other tribes to peace with the United States was signed on April 29, 1851, at Camp Barbour on the San Joaquin River. Poholeel, Ekeeno, Kayoya, Apemshee, and Chonohalma represented the tribe by making their "marks" on the document. The commissioners left Camp Barbour immediately to make treaties at other places in the state, leaving subagent Adam Johnston with the responsibility of supplying food for the numerous natives that had been gathered for the signing of the treaty and setting up the large, promised reservations. Two days after the commissioners left, in the midst of the turmoil, Major Savage appeared at Johnston's tent as commander of the Mariposa Battalion to "request" a license to trade with all of the Yokuts from the Chowchilla River to Kings River, fifty miles south. Johnston wisely delayed making a decision until June 20, but Savage was not going to wait.[6] He believed that there was a large amount of money to be made by putting the native people to work panning gold dust for him, so much money that he was willing to guarantee spending the $10,000 that was required by the government to buy farming tools, livestock, and food for the native people. He quickly revived the contacts with suppliers that had been dormant during the battalion fighting, and set up a trading post on the Fresno River near a large native encampment area and near the U.S. army contingent at Fort Miller.

---

5. The politicians knew that the strength of the nation depended partly upon the amount of the gold supporting the value of its currency. California was isolated from the then-existing United States, and it was possible that the state's citizens would declare it and its gold independent of the United States.

6. Crampton 1957:78–79; Phillips 1997:133–134.

Savage was never appointed as a government agent, but the Yokuts, the miners, and the U.S. Government treated him like one. Johnston started funneling livestock to him to feed the native people. For their part, the Chowchilla willingly accepted his control as warden of the reservation. He had, of course, saved them from starvation and annihilation, but there was also lasting animosity from the white invaders who thought that natives were not entitled to have the reservation land or to pan for gold. For the Chowchilla, Savage's status as leader of the battalion was believed to ensure their safety.

In the months that followed, Savage took his role as a trader and manager of the reservation seriously. According to his partner, Lorenzo Vinsonhaler, he provided medical help for native people and built a school for the children. While those claims may have been exaggerated, it is true that Savage used his knowledge of the Yokuts language to successfully teach the natives farming and ranching skills. The primary purpose of this education was to grow barley and wheat so he could make money by selling the grain to the army at the nearby fort, but he also used the grain to feed the people and allowed them to farm their own plots.[7]

Native people continued to arrive at the reservation in the months after it was begun. In some cases, white settlers and former miners pushed them off of their land, and in other cases native people were attracted from the hills by the food and protection they thought they would find on the reservation. However, this increase in the reservation's population and the late arrival of government funds caused food shortages. The people on the reservation became restless and began to doubt Savage's ability to feed and protect them. Three native boys sneaked into the reservation's corrals and killed John Bowling's horse to feed the people. Savage learned about this after the native people had a nice feast and flew into a rage. Savage saw that allowing such acts to occur unpunished conveyed a message to the native people that the horses vital for reservation operation also were available as food. In addition, it conveyed to the local white people as well as the natives that he did not have control of the reservation and its native people. For these reasons, he insisted the culprits be caught and punished. However, the natives that he spoke to would not tell him the names of the boys. Consequently, he formally demanded that the leaders of the tribes that were represented on the reservation turn over the guilty boys. This ploy produced more silence. After some time had passed, Savage called in some soldiers from the fort and arrested three of the native leaders, locking them

---

7. Phillips 1997:138.

up in the fort. Returning to the farm, he informed the native people that the chiefs would be released after the boys were punished. This message does not seem to have been well understood. Rather, this produced great anger among the native people on the reservation. Would their chiefs be locked up forever or even killed? All of the chiefs were revered elders, symbolic of their tribes, and it was a great insult to all of the people at the reservation that they were taken away. From their perspective, the act of stealing and eating a horse was so common in their history that it was not considered a criminal act.

It was during this incident that Poholeel emerged from the shadow of his deceased brother and became recognized as chief of the Chowchilla. As the brother of Jose Rey, all of the people looked toward him for leadership in resolving the conflict. As the threat of disruption and violence grew, Poholeel called for all warriors to assemble and to confront the fort with bows and arrows. This led to the soldiers and the nearby white people to overreact. An alarm was sent out directing all of the white people to leave their homes and go to the fort. The fort soldiers gathered weapons and prepared to repulse an attack. However, when the warriors arrayed themselves in front of the fort, Savage saw what the likely outcome of guns versus bows and arrows would be and wisely decided that the loss of a horse did not justify killing people. After talking to Poholeel, he ordered the release of the jailed chiefs.[8]

Thereafter Savage was seen by the Yokuts as a strong and just leader who could be counted on to support the native peoples. Poholeel and his family became close associates of Savage. He worked closely with Poholeel and began calling him "Blackhawk," after the great chief of the Sauk tribe in Illinois who, in 1832, led the Sauk and Fox warriors to fight the white immigrants who were taking the land of the natives. Savage had lived near the Sauk tribe and had admired the Sauk chief.

After learning about the stature of the chief in Illinois, Poholeel was honored by the name and, for the rest of his life, he was known as Chief Blackhawk.

Savage also developed a reputation as a defender of Yokuts people throughout the region. In August 1852, a conflict was brewing in the Kings River area where that river emerged from the mountains onto a fertile flatland. This land was the home of the Choinumne Yokuts, who we discussed in chapter 1, but a group of unscrupulous white men, led by a man named Walter Harvey, coveted the land and began moving onto it. Watoka, the

---

8. Phillips 1997:136–137.

Choinumne chief, then appealed to Savage for help in removing the white men from the tribe's land. Savage, however, was immersed in the problems of the Fresno reservation and did not go personally to help the Choinumne. Instead, he gave them a written document proclaiming that the land had been awarded to the Choinumne by the federal commissioners. Harvey ignored the document and gathered 25 armed men to go to Watoka's village, ostensibly to gain permission to take some of the land. After surrounding the village, Harvey tried to take Watoka prisoner, but, when this failed, he opened fire on the village people, killing 27 of them.[9]

When he heard of this outrage, Savage publicly denounced Harvey and rode south to the Kings River area on August 16, 1852, to prevent further bloodshed. By coincidence, Savage ran into Harvey at a river ferry and attacked him verbally and physically. Harvey was no match for the shorter but stronger man and Savage knocked him down twice. He soon realized that Savage was going to beat him badly. Desperately searching for some advantage, he noticed when Savage's handgun fell from his belt and was picked up and taken out of range by an observer. Harvey then pulled out his own gun and shot Savage three or four times, killing him instantly.[10]

The murder of Savage sent shock waves through the Yokuts tribes. Savage had long been known and revered by Yokuts people, even those who had never seen him. In May of that year, he had given a feast and had appeared before thousands of people from 12 Yokuts tribes and one Miwok tribe.[11] If any of them had doubted his support of the native people, this feast wiped all of that away and elevated him to a status above that of ordinary mortals. When he was killed, a Yokuts mourning ceremony that was held for him attracted thousands of the native people, and the wailing could be heard from a great distance.

Incredibly, Harvey was not held accountable for either the massacre of the Choinumne or for the murder of Savage.[12] Before Savage's murder, one of the commissioners, O. M. Wozencraft, appealed to the governor and the U.S. district attorney to have Harvey arrested and tried for the massacre, but the governor made no reply and the district attorney incredibly said the United States had no law that would apply to such massacres. Wozencraft continued to seek justice for the native people who were killed, but, in a surprising turn of events, Tulare County, where the massacre had taken

9. Phillips 1997:145–146; Hurtado 1988:115.
10. Bunnell 1880:251–253.
11. Phillips 1997:144–145.
12. Phillips 1997:149.

place, held an election for the position of county judge and Harvey won the election. Thereafter, no one tried to have Harvey punished.

Savage's reservation, never a political reality, gradually disintegrated. Lacking leadership, the food growing became ineffective and the native people began leaving the reservation for areas in which their traditional hunting and gathering methods could be used. Some Chowchillas reverted to raiding the white settlements: taking horses, mules, and cattle for food. Retaliatory raids by whites also resumed, attacking native people on and off the reservation,[13] and the level of violence between natives and whites soon returned to the level it had been before the treaties.[14]

However, unknown to anyone in California, significant changes had been made back in Washington regarding native people affairs several months before the events above occurred. On March 4, 1852, when the ratification of the treaties still looked like a possibility in Washington, U.S. President Fillmore had appointed Edward Beale, a friend of disgraced John Fremont,[15] to the post of Superintendent of Indian Affairs for California and had charged him with controlling the native people and changing them into farmers. Beale was a headstrong naval officer whose qualifications for the post were dubious at best.[16] He followed no one's orders but his own, and did not consult the commissioners or otherwise enlighten himself about reservation living conditions and needs.[17] Before going to California, he said it was not possible for the native people to benefit from schools or agriculture.[18] Later, however, he observed them at the Tejon Pass reservation cultivating their lands, and decided that reservation farms should be established in California. One of these, he proposed, would be 50,000 acres at Tejon Pass and another would be a very large tract between the San Joaquin and Fresno Rivers adjacent to the Chowchilla homeland.[19] Beale's plan was that the natives should have strict overseers and

---

13. Stockton *Journal*, Feb. 1853.

14. Phillips 2004:193–198.

15. Fremont had been court-martialed in 1847 (Hurtado 2006:208).

16. Phillips 2004:69.

17. When ordered by the Secretary of the Interior in 1853 to return to California by the fastest route (i.e., by ship), and while on the government payroll, he accepted employment in a private company planning the transcontinental railroad, arriving three months late in California. Phillips 2004:100–104.

18. Phillips 2004:72.

19. The Congress had specified that there be five reservations of no more than 25,000 acres apiece. The tract for the natives in the Fresno area was 30 miles downriver from Fort Miller and, according to Phillips, was 14 miles by 40 miles, or 358,400 acres. Since that amount of

be rewarded with food and shelter only if they worked hard at farming. They should support a military fort at each reservation, just as they had in the missions.[20] However, what Beale had failed to note was that the tribes represented at Tejon Pass had experienced mission life; they had been farming for many years and were accustomed to strict overseers. This would not be the case farther north. In addition, while the Tejon area was relatively free of insects, the Fresno area was not. After feeding the insects with futile farming for a few months, the original Fresno farm was abandoned in October 1853.[21]

Meanwhile, Beale continued to disregard directives from Washington regarding the organization and finances of native affairs in California. By the summer of 1854, his financial irregularities and insubordination had become intolerable to the Commissioner of Indian Affairs in Washington and, less than two years after he was appointed, Beale was dismissed.[22] Beale's ideas about and plans for the native people, however, were maintained. His replacement, Thomas Henley, postmaster of San Francisco, believed, as Beale did, that all good men were farmers and that a man will be lazy unless he is forced to work.[23] By September 1854, Henley was proceeding to implement Beale's plan to establish reservation farms and, over the next four years, he set up four farms in northern California and two farms in the south in addition to the Tejon farm.[24] Most of these were on land rented from white settlers. One of the southern farms, rented from Lorenzo Vinsonhaler, was adjacent to the large tract previously designated for a reservation by Beale in the Chowchilla territory.[25] This came to be called the Fresno Indian Farm. It consisted of about 500 acres on the Fresno River close to the town of Madera and about 50 miles west of Fort Miller, the nearest military base.

Such reservation farms were to be managed by government subagents, who reported directly to Henley. For the Fresno Farm, Henley appointed

land does not exist between the two rivers, it is likely that he meant 14 miles (the distance between the rivers) by 4 miles, or 35,840 acres. Phillips 2004:94.

20. Hurtado 1988:142; Phillips 2004:81.

21. Phillips 2004:104.

22. Hurtado 1988:144.

23. Phillips 2004:131.

24. Hurtado 1988:137.

25. Vinsonhaler had acquired the property at the time of the original Fresno farm. Since he was a trader like James Savage, it is likely that he acquired the property hoping to establish a trading post there, just as Savage had done farther up the Fresno. Phillips 2004:94, 148; Secrest 2003:165.

a man named Enyart, who, in turn, hired a heavy-handed farmer named Williams.[26] By November 1854, Enyart had gathered 440 natives willing to live on the farm, and from his reports to Henley, we know that 30 were Chowchilla led by Poholeel, now called Blackhawk; 220 were Chukchansi; and 190 were Miwoks.[27]

At first, things went well on Fresno Farm. Within three months, the native men had put in 300 acres of wheat and 350 acres of barley, fenced these fields, and built a few farm buildings. There were favorable rains and, in the spring of 1855, there were good wheat and barley harvests. This was fortunate because the government had stopped sending the treaty rations to the farm. With these harvests and game animals brought in by a native hunter, Enyart was able to keep the reservation fed and to report to Henley in April 1855 that the natives were in good condition.[28]

Problems began to develop on the farm, however. Williams was whipping the native people who, in his opinion, did not work hard enough. Then, in a confrontation, Williams killed a native in what he said was self-defense. As the native people began looking for him for revenge, he had to flee for his life to Fort Miller. Unhappy native groups began leaving the farm. Recognizing that the viability of the farm was in danger, Henley stepped in and dismissed Enyart.[29] M. B. Lewis, who had been assisting Enyart, was chosen to replace him as subagent of the farm in October 1855. This replacement would turn out to be of greatest importance to the Chowchilla. Lewis had served as adjutant to Savage in the Mariposa Battalion,[30] and he had developed great empathy for native people in that role. Evidence for this could be seen in Lewis's participation in the Mariposa Battalion. He had previously demonstrated his ability to fight native people when he led a cavalry unit against the Mexicans in Texas,[31] but he declined to fight against the Chowchillas and Yosemite Miwoks when the Mariposa Battalion was called upon to do so.[32]

Another change made by Henley at that time was less positive; instead of following the instructions from Washington that native people should have

26. Letter from Henley to Manypenny (Commissioner of Indian Affairs in Washington), Oct. 14, 1854; Phillips 2004:142–145.
27. Phillips 2004:143.
28. Phillips 2004:144.
29. Letter from Henley to Manypenny, April 3, 1856; Secrest 2002:219.
30. Crampton 1957:42.
31. Phillips 2004.
32. Bunnell 1880:98.

free choice about going to the reservations,[33] Henley decided that forced relocation by the state militia and federal troops must be used to get them onto the farms.[34] Eventually, all of California's reservations were to become military reservations.[35] Given the popular view of the Chowchilla and Chukchansi as dangerous horse thieves, it would not have been surprising if Henley had called out the soldiers from Fort Miller when even small problems developed at the Fresno Farm. With M. B. Lewis in charge, though, there was no need for force. By ensuring their safety and food resources, Lewis persuaded 300 additional natives to join the farm, bringing the total to approximately 700.[36]

M. B. Lewis tackled his work with great enthusiasm, organizing and instructing his charges in the development of the farm. The crops in fall 1855 were abundant.[37] By the following spring, however, M. B. Lewis's optimism had begun to evaporate. There were scanty winter rains and the 400 acres of wheat and 200 acres of barley that had been planted failed to mature.[38] Belatedly, Lewis realized irrigation of the farm was vital. He told the native men to dig an irrigation ditch from the Fresno River, but, when it was complete, the ditch failed to deliver enough water for more than a few of the planted acres. The Fresno River was never dependable, being reduced to a series of puddles in the summer sun. In addition, ground squirrels dug burrows in the banks of the ditch. The water was lost before it reached the fields.

Crops continued to be poor in succeeding years. The winter rains in 1856–57 and 1857–58 were again insufficient and the crops failed in both 1857 and 1858. In desperation, Lewis proposed and received permission to send the natives out to gather their own food.[39] Some were sent to the San Joaquin River to catch and dry salmon, while others were sent to the mountains to gather acorns. Ironically, the effort to turn the native people into farmers resulted in a confirmation of their traditional hunting and gathering way of life.

At the same time, conflicts between settlers and natives outside of the farm further impacted its viability. Settlers were raising large herds of pigs

---

33. Currie 1957:317.
34. Hurtado 1988:147.
35. Heizer 1978:704. Fresno River Farm became a military reservation in 1857, despite the absence of soldiers on the farm.
36. Phillips 2004:145.
37. Phillips 2004:148.
38. Letter from M. B. Lewis to Henley, Jan. 19, 1856.
39. Letter from Henley to M. B. Lewis, Aug. 7, 1856.

and allowing them to consume a large portion of the acorns under the oaks that were normally gathered by natives. The natives began killing some of the pigs when they came across them in the forests. Then the settlers, completely blind to the justice of the natives' slaughtering the pigs, formed vigilante gangs to drive the native people out of the forests. The conflict culminated in November 1858 when the vigilantes rounded up 250 natives—men, women, and children—and marched them, day and night, 70 miles from Tulare Lake to Fresno Farm, where they insisted that the Fresno Farm take them and guard them from returning to their homes. They stated unequivocally that the native people would be killed if they returned to their homes.[40] Lewis was, consequently, forced to purchase food to keep the refugees from starving to death. His funds eventually ran out and he had to take those able to walk to a wild area in the upper Kings River area where they had to fend for themselves.

With valiant efforts and self-sacrifice, M. B. Lewis kept the Fresno Farm alive by sending more and more groups out to forage for food. This made some of the natives happy because they thought that they would eventually be allowed to return to a traditional way of life. It was not to be. Despite Lewis's leadership and the labors of the native people, the farm became more and more unsustainable. Crops were never enough to feed the people on the farm and Lewis's funds were exhausted. The last blow came in 1859 when financial support from the U.S. Congress was quietly terminated. Lewis had sent many requests for funds to Henley's office, but time and time again they were perfunctorily answered without remittances and without explanation.[41] In June of 1859, Lewis had exhausted all of the farm's resources and was unable to pay the rent. Back in Washington, the last straw occurred when the 56th Congress canceled the official status of all of the farms.[42] Within a short period of time thereafter, the reservation farms in California were abandoned. Thousands of natives across the state found themselves evicted: homeless, destitute, and unprotected.

---

40. Phillips 2004:217; Hurtado 1988:153.
41. Letter from M. B. Lewis to Senator William Gwin Apr. 9, 1859.
42. Phillips 2004:221; Phillips 1997:189; end of government status recorded in the Congressional records: http://memory.loc.gov/ammem/amlaw/lwss-ilc.html.

8

The Failure of
the Fresno Farm

There were many reasons that the reservation farms failed, but the main reason was that Congress on the east coast of the continent did not fully understand the needs of the farm system that they themselves had authorized on the west coast, and, consequently, could not adequately fund the agents and subagents who were managing the farms, even if they were united in wanting to help the native people in the new state of California. It was necessary for the members of Congress to depend upon long-delayed, fragmentary, and biased reports. In addition, there were agents and subagents in California who, as we have seen, were only interested in lining their own pockets or were simply unprepared to manage a farm. To its credit, the Congress sent federal agents to assess the situation, but these individuals were poorly chosen and sent back garbled and inaccurate reports. By the end of the decade, with civil war looming, the members of Congress threw up their hands and canceled all funding. However, if we look more closely at the causes that led to the cancellation, we would be astounded to discover that the single, most instrumental cause was the reports were from a single federal agent who exaggerated the negative aspects of the reservation farms and ignored the positive: J. Ross Browne.

Browne was a man who loved to travel and to write about his travels.[1] He had no formal education, being homeschooled by his parents, but he developed beautiful handwriting and taught himself to write shorthand. With these skills, he was able to obtain a series of clerical positions, recording political activity for what later became the Congressional Record and performing secretarial duties in the Department of the Treasury. Shortly

1. Dillon 1965:4–5.

after beginning work at the Department of the Treasury, he was inexplicably promoted to be the personal secretary of the Secretary of the Treasury.[2] Although this employment lasted only a few months, he was later reemployed by the Secretary to act as a confidential agent and report on the many institutions and offices funded by the Department of the Treasury in the western states. In this capacity, he was told to root out and expose the failings of those employed at these institutions and offices, including those at the Office of Indian Affairs in California.[3]

As a writer and as a government agent, Browne always gave his audience what they wanted. When he wrote about his travels, he exaggerated what happened to make them sound more entertaining and exciting than they were. More important in the present context, when he was told to find graft and corruption in California, he found it everywhere, condemning people right and left regardless of the facts or circumstances that may have justified the actions of those he attacked. Some of those he condemned, perhaps most, were more victims of circumstance than the dishonorable villains he said they were. One of those he attacked became governor of California and another a state senator.[4]

In 1857, newspapers began publishing critical evaluations of Henley, calling for a complete auditing of his books,[5] and, as a result, Treasury assigned Browne the task of evaluating the system. The Department of the Interior also sent a second agent, Godard Bailey, to investigate the situation, and over the next year they visited offices and reservations, at least sometimes together. However, the conclusions that they drew from their investigations were radically different. Bailey blamed the difficulties experienced by the reservation system on the system itself, stating that it was simply not in the nature of things for the natives to work on property that was not their own. Nevertheless, he could not propose an alternative system and recommended that reservations in the Central Valley be continued with a minimum number of white agents supervising.[6] Browne, however, found corruption at every level of the system. Henley, he said, could not account for the funds he had received and must have been using government funds for himself rather sending it to the reservations. Further, he

---

2. Dillon 1965:8–9.
3. Secretary of the Treasury James Guthrie was developing a reputation as "a ruthless reformer . . . weeding out incompetency" (Dillon 1965:17).
4. Dillon 1965:23, 51.
5. Phillips 2004:230.
6. Phillips 2004:232–233.

decided without evidence that all of the subagents at the reservation farms were also defrauding the government by using reservation property and the labor of native people for their own private gain.[7] Browne stopped short of recommending that the system be abandoned, but he said it would work only if honest men could be found to run it.[8]

When he visited the reservations and farms, he appears to have already made up his mind that he would only find incompetence and cheating. On the Fresno Farm, for example, he found about 50 natives there instead of the reported 350. M. B. Lewis explained that he had not received sufficient funds to feed the natives in his charge and that, as a consequence, he had to let the missing natives go out to forage for acorns and catch salmon to feed the farm population and to prepare for the coming winter. Browne dismissed this explanation as subterfuge and reported that Lewis was lying to conceal his misuse of government property and money. Had Browne collected evidence with an open mind, he would have found that farming in that area was heavily dependent upon winter rains and that the farm functioned well only when there was adequate rain, as in the winter of 1854–55. Such critical factors seem to have been unimportant to him. The subagents should have overcome such factors. In a letter to the Commissioner of Indian Affairs in Washington, Browne stated that he could not understand why the subagents could not make the natives become farmers when

> . . . a few Jesuit (*sic*) missionaries in a wild and savage country with nothing to depend upon but their own energy and sagacity, built up extensive missions, cultivated immense fields, planted vineyards and orchards, raised innumerable herds of cattle, supported and fed in abundance whole tribes of Indians, brought in peace without bloodshed under their control, and made a handsome revenue to maintain their religious system.[9]

Browne's reports, accusing all of the people involved in the reservation system of incompetence and malfeasance, were greeted with alarm in Washington, and Godard Bailey's report was taken as confirmation of Brown's conclusions.[10] The net result was that Browne's reports were taken as fact and the reservation system was defunded. New reservations

---

7. Rawls 1984:157.
8. Hurtado 1988:150.
9. Report of J. R. Browne to the Commissioner of Indian Affairs, Sept. 18, 1858. Browne had traveled up and down the state from mission to mission and failed to discover, among other things, that the priests had been Franciscans, not Jesuits.
10. Hurtado 1988:150.

would be brought into being later, but the government had proven to the native people once again that it could not be depended upon to sustain and protect them. For the Chowchilla, like many other tribes, there was only one answer, namely, to accept a marginalized existence within white society and to be as anonymous as possible.

J. Ross Browne is still praised by some authors for tearing the reservation system apart, proclaiming, as did historian James Rawls, that Browne had done the native people a service by exposing Henley and the subagents as "incompetent and venal."[11] However, the inconsistencies and exaggerations in Browne's reports show this calumny for what it is, a broad-brush condemnation of all for the sins of a few. There is no doubt that there was some mismanagement in the system and significant exploitation of the natives, but little is said by Browne's admirers about the dedication and generosity of subagents like M. B. Lewis or about the thousands of natives who were left unprotected and starving as the result of Browne's own incompetence. While the farms existed, there was a legal barrier protecting the natives who came to the farms from the exploitation and violence of ethnocentric white men. Thanks to J. Ross Browne, that barrier was removed. Without the safe harbors that the farms represented, alcoholism, disease, and violence against natives in the succeeding years increased dramatically.

M. B. Lewis had foretold what would happen when the natives left the Fresno Farm. Writing to the Superintendent of Indian Affairs in San Francisco three years earlier, Lewis was particularly concerned about the transmission of syphilis. Tantalized by food, fancy dress, and trinkets, he said, young native women would submit to white men who offered these in exchange for sex. Then, when other tribal members learned of this illicit sex, the women would become the

> ... sport and traffic of worthless Indian men. In one or two brief years they [will] become diseased and at the age of twenty wear the features of thirty-five to forty; outcasts among their own people; and as a general thing before they arrive at the age of thirty, die a shameful and miserable death.[12]

Lewis would live to see it happen in many tribes. In 1859, after the Fresno Farm closed, he was asked to give a report for the Washington office regarding the location and condition of tribes that had been in some way

---

11. Rawls 1984:156–157.
12. Letter from M. B. Lewis to T. Henley July 22, 1856.

associated with the farm. Of the 22 tribes that he listed, he identified 13 that were "unhealthy" or "dying out" as the result of alcohol and disease or as the result of being driven away from their land and food resources.[13] These 13 tribes were not living on and protected by the farm; they were scattered among the ongoing flood of white immigrants. For them, the threat of extinction was very real.

There were some natives for whom tribal identity remained strong because their leaders were strong. When the Fresno Farm failed, these groups returned to their homelands, if that was possible, or, if not, gathered in unoccupied areas near their homelands. The Chukchansi went to an area that was part of their homeland in the headwaters of the Fresno and San Joaquin Rivers, and, similarly, the Pitkachi moved back across the San Joaquin River to land that they identified as their own. The Pohonichi Miwoks, however, were blocked by mining activity from returning to their own homelands, and so moved to the upper Chowchilla River to settle near their traditional homeland.[14] Their new area was previously part of the Chowchilla homeland that had been vacated during the Mariposa War when Jose Rey moved his people for protection deep into the Sierra Mountains, on the headwaters of the San Joaquin beyond the Chukchansi homeland.[15] Some of the Chowchilla may have accompanied the Pohonichi to the upper Chowchilla River. In the early years of the twentieth century, when anthropologists were trying to collect information about the cultures of native people, two villages were found there. One of these, found by Merriam in 1902, was a small group of related Chowchillas and the other village, found by Kroeber, was named "Chowchilla" but was occupied by Pohonichi people.[16]

Although some Chowchilla may have sought refuge in the mountains, the core of the tribe, led by Blackhawk, stayed in the Fresno Farm area for two more years with the help of M. B. Lewis. His funds, however, dwindled rapidly and, at the end of that period, there seemed to be no hope that the group could remain united. It was almost miraculous for them that Abraham Lincoln signed the Homestead Act in 1861.[17] This act stipulated

---

13. Report of M. B. Lewis to the Commissioner of Indian Affairs, Jun. 15, 1859.
14. Kroeber suggests that the Pohonichi were not a tribe (Kroeber 1925:443), but Gayton's later data regarding intermarriage with the Chukchansi suggests that they were (Gayton 1948:194–196).
15. Now occupied by the Mono people.
16. Kroeber 1925:443; Merriam field notes 1902.
17. Public Law 37-64, May 20, 1862.

Figure 9. Mary Blackhawk Lewis (1828–1907)

Figure 10. Thomas Lewis (1830–1895), son of M. B. Lewis and Mary Blackhawk's husband

that anyone who had not opposed the United States with force of arms could claim 160 acres of public land and, by living on the land and improving it, could gain title to the land. There was great commotion in the mother lode region about the promises of this act among former miners and other white immigrants, and M. B. Lewis realized that, although Blackhawk and his family were technically ineligible, he could use this act for them. After a quick search for an appropriate site, Lewis claimed 160 acres on a tributary of Willow Creek near what is now the town of O'Neals. Other than the availability of water from the intermittent stream and a spring, it is not known why he chose this property. It was about five miles southeast of the Fresno River in Chukchansi territory. Perhaps there was competition from other homesteaders. In any case, it was away from white settlements and, at the invitation of Lewis, it became the new home of the followers and family of Chief Blackhawk.

It may seem curious that M. B. Lewis was willing to go to such lengths to help the Chowchilla. From the beginning of Lewis's tenure as subagent

Figure 11. Blackhawk Mountain near Chief Blackhawk's homestead

for the Fresno Farm, he had worked closely with Chief Blackhawk's people, more as a coworker than a leader, and his letters demonstrate that he respected and trusted them. However, there were other reasons for Lewis's desire to help the Chowchilla. During his early association with the farm in 1854, his son, Thomas Lewis, had become attached to Mary Blackhawk, the daughter of Jose Rey and niece of Chief Blackhawk, and, by the time the Fresno Farm closed, they had married in the Chowchilla manner and had a baby girl.[18] With the Lewis and Blackhawk families solidly linked, it was natural that they would come together to permanently settle on or near the Lewis homestead. It is also likely that other Chowchilla came with the two families to the Lewis homestead; 160 acres was large enough for many homes. However, from later records, we are only certain that Blackhawk's and Mary Blackhawk Lewis's families went to with M. B. Lewis to his homestead.

By 1884, when M. B. Lewis died, Mary Blackhawk's children and grandchildren numbered more than 20, not counting spouses, and more land was needed. Blackhawk then applied for a homestead and two years later, despite the clause in the Homestead Act that recipients could not have

---

18. According to Mary Blackhawk Lewis's Land Allotment Affidavit, dated Apr. 26, 1897, they were also married in 1864 or 1865. The birth of this daughter is indicated on the 1928 role applications of Jane Romero, Carmelita Topping, and Caroline Lewis Castro, but the child's name is not given.

opposed the United States with force of arms, acquired a homestead for himself and his descendants about a mile west of the Lewis homestead. This might have created a division of the Chowchillas, but Mary Blackhawk, then 47, played an important role in holding the two homestead groups together, and when Blackhawk died five years later, she became the tribal leader as the eldest survivor of the chief's lineage and as the owner of Lewis's homestead. She was to continue as the leader of the Chowchilla for 22 years, until her death in 1913. During their 60 years of leadership, deceased members of M. B. Lewis's and Blackhawk's families, including M. B. Lewis himself, were brought to their homesteads for burial. Although few nonnative people now know the connection, the 2,000-foot mountain behind the two homesteads was given the name Blackhawk Mountain, a fitting memorial to them all.

9

The Ghost Dance of 1869

Working within and from the homesteads, the Chowchilla reestablished a hunting and gathering way of life, but added some of the farming and gardening methods they had learned at the Fresno Farm. Their homesteads thus became workable hybrids of Chowchilla and white subsistence methods. Finding and producing enough food, however, was still not an easy task. The local creek flowed only during the wet times of the year and the summer heat limited the crops. There were a few springs that ran all year, however, and with these the Chowchilla were able to establish a viable, if difficult, way of life and their population began to grow. While other tribes were disappearing into the margins of white society or dying for lack of adequate food and medical assistance, the number of children born to the Chowchilla increased steadily throughout the last four decades of the nineteenth century. The possession of the homesteads was a key element in their prosperity, just as the ownership of a defined homeland had provided prosperity before the foreigners arrived. It gave them security, stability, and optimism. Owning property also gave them some flexibility in their identity and their cultural adaptation to the environment. By keeping to themselves while outwardly displaying what looked like an American farm, they could maintain their own culture and avoid conflicts with neighbors who might harbor fear or hatred of native people.

However, for the native people who were forced off of the defunct farms with nowhere to go, the circumstances were very different and very frightening. They had no way of protecting or even feeding themselves. Because there were no places where they could come together as tribes, they tended to break up into smaller groups based upon village or family ties, groups that moved frequently, trying to find food and safety in the context of white greediness and selfish disregard. Incidents of cruelty and exploitation by white people continued to happen without opprobrium. Disease was more common among landless natives who could not avoid contact with people they did not know. Malaria, syphilis, smallpox, diphtheria, pneumonia, measles, dysentery, and tuberculosis all continued to circulate in native populations[1] lacking medical assistance. Even when a native doctor was available, disease was very demoralizing because the Yokuts held a traditional belief that diseases were thrown through the air by their enemies, including white people. Then, as they grew more desperate, anger and resentment among native people living together, sometimes ignited by alcoholism, scattered them into even smaller groups, undermining the sharing and cooperation that could ameliorate their problems.[2]

Under these horrible conditions, it is not a surprise that the landless native people sought supernatural help, which they thought would erase white cruelty and exploitation while restoring their traditional ways of life. When a messiah emerged among them in 1869, most of the native people happily welcomed him and fervently believed his message. The messiah was a Paiute prophet named Tavibo who proclaimed that a new world order would soon appear. For the Yokuts, Tavibo's vision revealed a future time when Tuwawiya, the Yokuts' Ruler of the Dead, would return to earth and bring back all the people who had died since the white people arrived. Then there would be no more sickness and death. The white people would disappear, leaving their possessions for the native people. Game animals, salmon, and acorns would be abundant again and the generosity of nature would know no end. There was, however, one big condition: All of this would happen only if the majority of the people in each tribe danced and sang special songs that would be provided by the prophet. If most of a tribe danced and sang as instructed but others did not, the nonbelievers would be turned into logs when the great transformation came to pass.[3]

Tavibo's vision was a powerful one and his religion, called the Ghost Dance religion, spread with amazing rapidity to all tribes in all directions from Tavibo's home in Walker Lake, Nevada. Within a year, it was passed from tribe to tribe through all of the tribes north and south from Nevada. To the north, it circled the Sierra Nevada Mountains, across the top of California to the Karok and Yurok in the northwest corner of the state and then south to the Wintun, Pomo, and other tribes in the Coast Ranges and

---

1. Cook 1955, 1976a.
2. Gray 1993:211. Wallace (1956; 1965) provides an excellent analysis that explains such lamentable dysfunctional behavior between people who were all being exploited by an outside group.
3. Gayton 1930:66.

the Sacramento Valley.[4] In the same year, the message went south from Walker Lake through the Owens Valley Paiute and over the Sierras to the North Fork Mono near the Chowchilla and the Chukchansi.[5]

A Mono chief at North Fork named Joijoi became the local disciple of Tavibo and traveled back and forth to Walker Lake several times to visit the prophet. After he had learned all of the songs and dances, Joijoi announced a big dance on a tabletop mountain near North Fork so that all of the believers west of the Sierras could learn them. Runners were sent by Joijoi to invite people from all tribes and the response was amazing. Large numbers of natives came from all directions. So many of them attended that they ran out of food before the prescribed six nights of dancing and singing were over. With the exertion of dancing and the unplanned fasting, many dancers experienced visions of the wonders to come. Then, after the dances ended, the representatives of each tribe went home to teach others so that they, too, would see the new world.[6]

This emotional activity was swirling around the Chowchilla for three years. However, according to their descendants, the Chowchilla connected with the homesteads did not participate in the new religion.[7] They had food and protection and had no reason to desire that M. B. Lewis and his non-native family would be killed. In contrast, tribes on all sides of the Chowchilla fell under the Ghost Dance spell.[8] Yokuts from the Lakisamne in the north to the Chunut in the south adopted the religion.[9] After three years of dancing, however, doubters began to emerge. None of the ancestors had returned and sickness and death showed no sign of abating. Gradually, the followers of the religion lost belief in the promised salvation and stopped dancing and singing. By 1875, six years after it had started, the Ghost Dance was completely abandoned.[10]

The natives blamed themselves for the failure. The dance was not done right, they said, and not enough natives had danced.[11] Their beliefs had buoyed them up for a few years, but the failure of the Ghost Dance plunged

---

4. Du Bois 1939:1–3.

5. Gayton 1930:60–61.

6. Gayton 1930:66–68.

7. Other native communities (e.g., the Mountain Maidu) also heard about the vision and saw the dances but did not adopt the new religion (Du Bois 1939:39).

8. Bean and Vane 1978:662 (map).

9. Gray 1993:208; Latta 1949:244–250.

10. Gayton 1930:62. The son of Tavibo, Wovoka, caused renewed interest in the Ghost Dance in 1890. This later form of the Ghost Dance was also widely adopted for a while. It swept eastward and was being performed when the massacre at Wounded Knee occurred.

11. Latta 1949:247–250.

them back into hopelessness. Social conditions of some of the natives became even worse than they had been before the Ghost Dance because individuals faithful to Tavibo had, logically, forsaken employment at white ranches and businesses in anticipation of the world renewal. Other individuals neglected their families and squandered resources that were vital to their existence. Whole tribes became so mired in despair that they sank into a state so disorganized and so self-destructive that they ceased to exist within a decade after the collapse of Tavibo's movement. One case of this was that of the Lakisamne, the Chowchilla's neighbor to the northwest who lived along the Stanislaus River. This tribe had once gained fame and power under renowned chief Jose Jesus in the 1840s. However, five years after the end of the Ghost Dance, a state assemblyman named L. C. Branch visited them and was shocked to find how far the Lakisamne had fallen. Disease, alcoholism, and violence had become so widespread and so common that he wrote this terrible prophecy:

> Disease has made such inroads upon them that it is but reasonable to expect that the few remaining will soon waste away and perish from the land. As a race, they are no longer recognized; their huts are deserted; their strength is broken; their women are diseased; their men have lost the vigor and manhood of their fathers; the germs of disease are sown in the children, and in another decade it will be hard to find one among them to tell the tale of his race.[12]

The Lakisamne Yokuts, indeed, became so fragmented that they ceased to exist as a society shortly thereafter. By the beginning of the twentieth century, Kroeber could find no one in the area—native or non-native—who knew who they were.[13]

Fortunately, the Chowchilla who recognized the leadership of Chief Blackhawk and Mary Blackhawk Lewis avoided this fate. Their tribal land base consisting of M. B. Lewis' homestead was legally recognized and respected by the whites. Perhaps just as important, they had developed a strongly self-reliant philosophy of life. They did not envy the whites their material possessions. Believing that what they had was all they needed, they lived quiet, self-sacrificing lives. Today, a visit to their now-abandoned houses in the hills shows Chowchilla descendants the Spartan nature of their ancestors' lives, lives that evoke great pride in their tribal inheritance.

---

12. Branch 1881:94, quoted in Gray 1993:211–212.
13. Gray 1993:214.

10

Missionaries, Boarding Schools and Allotments

For 80 years, from 1850 to 1930, Americans believed that, if the country's native people stopped being "Indian" and adopted the "American" way of life, they would naturally become part of American society. The wars and atrocities that occurred in the western states were unfortunate events but they were the fault of the native people who were obstinately refusing to give up their traditional ways of life. These dreadful conflicts would continue until they adopted family-based agriculture and American capitalism.

These beliefs became the standard doctrine for Americans after the Gold Rush. Then, after Darwin's ideas were published in 1859, academicians in the social sciences thought they saw a scientific basis for that doctrine: Human societies evolve just as animals evolve. This erroneous validation filtered down to ordinary Americans along with a very poor understandings of Darwin's ideas. The general reaction to Darwinian ideas was heard from the clergy, namely, that his ideas were blasphemous and evil. But educated Americans were gradually brought around to believe, as the academicians did, that Darwin's ideas referred to *cultural* evolution as well as to biological evolution, and just as biological evolution had created human beings as the top of the animal kingdom, cultural evolution had created Christian Anglo-Saxon society at the absolute pinnacle of social evolution. Most notable were the books of Lewis Henry Morgan, a New York State Senator who had studied the Iroquois natives, and Edward B. Tylor, a professor at Oxford. These writers expanded the concept of cultural evolution by claiming that societies evolve through three stages: savagery (i.e., hunting and gathering people), barbarism (i.e., herders of animals), and civilization (best represented by current Anglo-Saxon civilization). All societies must climb this *unilineal* ladder of cultural evolution, they thought.[1] Thus, they concluded that the Chowchilla and all other hunters and gathers were "savages" and would want to become more evolved when they saw the superiority of American society. As late as 1919, Fresno County historian Paul Vendor described the Chowchilla and other Yokuts as still being on "the lowest scale of development."[2]

Today it is clear that there are several things very wrong about the theory of unilineal cultural evolution. Anyone who has read even a few ethnographies knows that (1) all cultures do not change in the same way; (2) progress is not inevitable and cannot be defined in terms of how people get their food alone; (3) the idea that a pinnacle society exists or could be achieved is a delusion: and (4) criticizing a society by comparison with another society is never valid. Nevertheless, unilineal thinking prevailed in the public and governmental perception of native tribes until about 1930.

Although the concept of unilineal evolution remained as the basic doctrine for the populace through this eighty-year period, there was continual argument about whether or not natives could "improve," or, if so, whether Americans could or should help or push the native people "up the ladder." The first modification in the thinking about native/non-native relations that became widespread was that Christianity should be used as a lure for future help and forgiveness. Indigenous people should be converted to Christianity first, then other problems could be worked out. President Grant championed this idea. Shortly after his inauguration in 1868 he proclaimed that one of his main objectives would be to protect the native people for this purpose, and during his first term he pushed for larger reservations. Efforts to protect and convert the natives would be futile if they were scattered across the landscape. This escalation of reservations produced early enthusiasm from both natives and non-natives, but by 1872 Grant was receiving negative reports. Getting the natives from different tribes to settle in one area was easier said than done. Grant believed that the main cause for this was that many of the Indian Agents on the reservations were active army officers who had led attacks against the natives. Consequently, with the help of the Congress, he disqualified army officers from serving as Indian Agents and established the "Peace Policy," which called for Indian Agents on all reservations to be Christian missionaries

---

1. Morgan *Ancient Societies* 1877; Tylor *Primitive Culture* 1871.
2. Vendor 1919:65.

from prominent Christian churches. In particular, Quakers were given 16 reservations; Methodists 14; Presbyterians 9; Episcopalians 8; Roman Catholics 7; Baptists 5; Dutch Reformed 5; Congregationalists 3; Christian Church 2; Unitarians 2; Lutherans 1; and The Board of Commissioners for Foreign Missions 1.[3] The policy further established that these sponsoring churches would be responsible for choosing the missionaries and for reorganizing life on the reservations to accomplish conversions.

The Peace Policy was abandoned in 1881. During that period, it became apparent that letting each of the sponsoring churches operate independently with its own organization and methods, while the government funded and supplied them all, produced an out-of-control bureaucratic nightmare. The only solution was for Congress and the BIA to take control again. All Indian Agents should report to the BIA, not to different church organizations. In addition, continued incidents like Custer's debacle at Little Bighorn in 1876 convinced the Congress that army units should be stationed at each reservation to protect the people and fight the natives if necessary. For these reasons, the BIA moved in the early 1880s to replace missionary agents with agents who would use a more forceful, militaristic approach to control or eliminate native cultures.

Nevertheless, despite the drastic reduction of the influence of the churches on governmental relations with the native people, the number of missionaries engaged in proselytizing among native populations increased. This was the result of missionaries moving from reservations into small towns and finding that they had more success among nonreservation natives, where government policies and agents did not interfere as much.[4] There were also many more places for missionaries to work, not only because there were many small towns, but also because BIA policy did not inhibit multiple missionaries from different religions working in the same towns, as it did before. In the area of the Chowchilla homeland, the Presbyterian and Baptist missionaries were very active using two different approaches.[5] The Presbyterians bought land in the town of North Fork, not far from the Lewis homestead, and built a church and boarding school for native children. The Baptists, on the other hand, built several small places for worship in the towns of Coarsegold, Friant, Cold Springs, Dunlap, and

---

3. Higham 2000:120–121; Rawls 1984:158–161; Utley 1984:127–133.
4. There were four reservations that may have been involved in this movement, two in California (Round Valley and Tule River) and two in Nevada, just on the other side of the state boundary (Walker Ranch and Pyramid Lake).
5. Plains 1991:48.

Auberry on unclaimed native land so that they did not have to buy land themselves. The Baptist plan was to go to the natives wherever they were, instead of asking the natives to come into a central place. By making their missionaries peripatetic, the Baptists could cover the area more thoroughly than the Presbyterians. When the two Protestant groups established themselves in the same area, a competition developed to see which denomination could baptize the most natives, regardless of whether those that were baptized became church members or not. It was a mechanism that made the two groups more eager to find native people and persuade them, in one way or another, to be baptized. This competition and the two approaches tell us that the missionaries of these and other churches combed the Chowchilla area thoroughly for converts.

The storm of Protestant evangelism, however, had little effect upon the Chowchillas because they identified with the Catholic religion. This affiliation stems, according to Jerry Brown, the current tribal chairman, from the late 1830s, when many Chowchilla were incarcerated in San Juan Bautista Mission, where they were baptized, given Spanish names, and indoctrinated in the Catholic religion. The only evidence that I have concerning this matter is that Jose Rey and Jose Juarez came back with their Spanish names and did not revert to their native names. This contrasts with what other Yokuts leaders did. When the treaty with the federal commissioners was signed in 1851, 56 important men represented 14 Yokuts tribes. Of these, only five men were using Spanish names.

In the last two decades of the nineteenth century, when the Protestants were pursuing every possible native convert, it is likely that claiming Catholic affiliation gave the Chowchilla people an escape from Protestant attention and white society generally. In addition, the Chowchilla people were still living in fear of retribution from white people who had lived there at the time of the Mariposa War. For that reason, too, they kept a low profile. This is indicated by the federal census of natives in Madera County in 1910, in which no natives were recorded as living in or around the homesteads. That area was apparently overlooked by census workers, perhaps thinking that no native people lived there. The Chowchilla community, nevertheless, was functioning and growing at the time. Three descendants of Jose Rey were born that year. In 1928, when the Chowchilla had reason to believe that their years of hiding were over, 76 self-identified Chowchillas of all ages were found by census takers to be living in the homestead area.[6]

---

6. 1928 Indian Survey records, San Bruno, CA.

Figure 12. Isolated Chowchilla cabin occupied during the Chowchilla reclusive years at the end of the 19th century

The reclusive nature of Chowchilla life also saved many of their children from the torture of boarding schools. While the Protestant missionaries were scouring California for converts, the congressmen back in Washington no longer believed that missionaries were able to acculturate natives. Reports from the missionaries in the west and the churches they represented spoke of great numbers of baptisms and native church members,[7] but these reports were hard to verify and subsequent reports usually revealed substantial exaggerations. Verified data that indicated acculturation—e.g., number of native farms or permanent family dwellings—was virtually nonexistent. Consequently, the congressmen came to the conclusion that natives had to be forced to become "civilized," whether they wanted to or not.

During the 1880s, the Congress pursued two tactics to force the natives to "improve": One tactic focused upon education and the other on land ownership. The first tactic was developed in 1882 when the congressmen learned about a boarding school for native children in Carlisle, Pennsylvania, run by a former army officer named Pratt. By treating his native students as if they were military recruits, forced to believe whatever their leaders told them, Pratt claimed that his students gave up all semblance of native culture by the time they graduated. The congressmen were very impressed

---

7. See Cornelia Taber, *California and Her Indian Children*, for examples of such reports.

by Pratt's claims and made a dramatic shift in national policy to emphasize the construction of boarding schools with *mandatory* attendance of all native children. This was made the law in 1891.

One appalling aspect of the new policy was that it legalized kidnapping. Schools for natives that did *not* require the students to stay at the schools did not have any lasting effect on the natives. Mandatory enrollment, on the other hand, would have great effect, but it would necessitate sending law officials to the dwellings of native families and physically taking children away from their parents and keeping them away for years. We can only speculate about why the incredible immorality of this did not matter to the congressmen. They were spending a lot of money on native affairs and the new policy would save money that could be spent on other, non-native items in the budget. Natives would not go to war if their children were effectively locked up in a government school. Further, building the schools would not cost much because only three or four schools could serve an entire state. Once a child was taken from his or her parents, it really didn't matter how far the child was taken, and, hence, only a few schools would be needed.

In California, five boarding schools were built at Tule River, Round Valley, Hoopa, Middleton, and Perris[8] to serve the entire state. Later this was reduced to only three schools: Sherman Indian School in Riverside (opened 1892 and still open), Greenville, in the northern Sierras (opened 1890, closed 1923), and Fort Bidwell, located far from anywhere in the extreme northeast corner of the state (opened 1890, closed 1930). The children of Chowchilla families who were rounded up and forcibly taken were transported to Sherman Indian School in Riverside more than 240 miles south of the homesteads.

As I mentioned above, the Chowchilla's reclusiveness may have saved many Chowchilla children from going to a boarding school. Perhaps some of the Chowchilla families were able to move higher in the foothills and avoided discovery. The families on or near the homesteads, however, remained there, maintaining the outward appearance of an American homestead with their housing and gardens and using English family names. One set of data suggests that about half of the Chowchilla children avoided being forced to go to Sherman. That set of data is a complete and informative roster of children at Sherman for 1910. This roster includes 26 Mono

---

8. Castillo 1978:116. Later they found that there was not enough water at Perris and the school was transferred to Riverside.

children, 15 Chukchansi children, but only six Chowchilla children, who were still hiding behind the subterfuge of being Mariposas.[9] Chowchilla genealogies show that there were at least 19 Chowchilla children of school age in 1910.[10]

The second tactic introduced in the 1880s and based on unilineal thinking was the promise of land if the natives would live like Americans. Like all unilineal thinking, this was ethnocentric; if Americans like to own land for our families, the natives must want to own land, too. In 1887, Senator Henry Dawes of Massachusetts guided a law through Congress called the Dawes Allotment Act. This proposed that the government divide up all of the reservation land and give it back to the natives as family-owned plots called allotments. Since this would take away the communal property that defined the tribe, he thought, the tribe would become dysfunctional and families would have to survive on their own as American families do. All of this was dead wrong. But, right or wrong, "leftover" land on the reservations after the allotments would be purchased from the tribe by the government, at a price determined by the government, and given to white settlers or the railroads.

The real reason for the law was to support and extend the economic base of the United States. The natives would indeed be given land allotments, but only if they jumped many hurdles. First, the allotted land would remain the property of the government ("in the public trust") for 25 years before the title was transferred to the allottee. During that time, the allottee and his family were expected to improve the land by raising crops and building a house. When the title was transferred to the allottee, the land would be conveyed by "patent in fee simple," which meant that it would be put on the real estate tax roles, assessed at the value of the improved property. If the allottee could not pay the taxes, the land could be sold for the taxes. In practice, the land was never owned by the allottee, except in cases where the land had no economic value. While the land was being "held in trust" for 25 years, a government agent could judge whether or not the allottee was competent by American standards. If the allottee was judged incompetent, the agent would take control of the land and lease it to a white man or put the land up for sale. At the end of the 25-year period, the agent could also decide whether or not an allottee was competent to sell the allotted property, and if not, he would arrange to have the land sold at auction

---

9. The tribal identity of four children on the list was not given.
10. The roster is online at www.mariposaresearch.net.

for the native. Thus, the primary effect of the law was not to isolate native families and change them into farmers but, rather, to destroy the tribes and take land away from natives and give it to white people—or, at least, to some particular white people. Some allotment land ultimately became privately owned land for railroads and power lines, for example. When the allotment program ended in 1936,[11] white people owned 91 million acres, or 65 percent, of the land that had been presumably reserved for native people.[12]

The Chowchilla, of course, were not in any way connected to a reservation. For nonreservation natives, the Dawes Act stated that they could apply for pieces of "public" land in amounts similar to the allocations given to reservation natives. Since the details of the allotment program were not known, several Chowchilla families applied for allotments of land, hoping to get back at least some of their traditional homeland. They did not see allotments as a threat to their traditional way of life; rather, they saw allotments as a way of reinstating their hunting and gathering to some degree. They were nevertheless skeptical about the program because, after all, the government had promised to give them land before, in the 1851 treaties, and had failed to fulfill their promises. It was a happy surprise that this time the government did indeed give land allotments to isolated Chowchilla families, and, after 25 years, gave some of these families title to their allotments. However, requests for allotment plots that white men wanted were commonly denied and the natives who made these requests were given land that was chosen by the BIA agents without consideration of the location of the Chowchilla homeland, the needs of the families, the accessibility of the plots, or whether there was water on the property. For this reason, we are not surprised to learn that very few Chowchilla families now live on land that they received as an allotment.

There were two other major flaws in the Allotment Act. One of these was that there was no mention of how and by whom native land rights were to be enforced, and the other was that there was no process by which allotments could be sold or given by the allottee to other natives. The Act was meant to prevent tribal ownership, and if allottees were able to sell or give their allotments to other natives, it was theoretically possible for tribes to accumulate land later and reestablish the tribal land base. We are forced

---

11. Rawls 1984:211. Allotment continued in Alaska until 1993!
12. Debo 1970:331. This is remarkably similar to the secularization of the missions in the 1830s when the local haciendas grabbed the land intended for the native people.

to conclude that the Act was never intended to give land back to native people. The intent of the Act was, in fact, the opposite: to disinherit the natives of their own land and to arrange for reservation land to be bought and sold like other non-native land. It may be cynical to say that by putting BIA agents—who lived isolated without oversight—in charge of every step of the allotment process, Dawes and other supporters knew they were putting the fox in the henhouse.

In the years from 1887 and 1926, the amount of corruption among the BIA Agents and land speculators grew incredibly. Finally, the Department of the Interior commissioned the independent Brookings Institute to form a committee, led by Lewis Merriam, to visit reservations, communities, agencies, hospitals, and schools that served native people and, in doing so, evaluate the social and economic conditions of the native people.[13] Merriam was a highly educated lawyer who understood government administration and operations. He and his team of experts conducted fieldwork in 23 states, including California and, in particular, the Chowchilla homeland. Merriam was the one who found Chowchilla people living on the upper Mariposa Creek. After three years of preparation, Merriam's report, called "The Problem of Indian Administration," was given to the Hoover administration and published. In it, the BIA and the Congress were both found to be guilty of the outrageous theft or swindle of land that had been given or set aside for the native people. Boarding schools, health facilities and services, and the allotment program were heavily criticized and condemned. As a result, boarding schools were closed or modified. The elementary grades at Sherman were eliminated and the school reduced to a high school. A program for the improvement of the medical facilities and services was begun. Unfortunately, the allotment program was not immediately terminated or even modified because the legal entanglements of allotment ownership, transfer, and sale were so complicated that the legislators refused to deal with the issue. Another four years went by before the allotment program was terminated, and during that time an additional 800 square miles of land were allotted.

---

13. Debo 1970:336., Merriam 1928, Wikipedia: Merriam Report.

11

Rancherias and
the IRA: 1900–1950

As white settlers and land speculators usurped more and more land in the United States, the number of homeless and destitute natives steadily increased, particularly in California. Native families were commonly observed camping on the private property of white people and asking for help and food at the backdoors of white residences. While some white families heartlessly scorned the natives, others appealed to churches and the government to help the native people. One group that came forward to help was the Northern California Indian Association (NCIA), a Protestant group that was founded in 1894 in San Jose. This group helped by gathering donations in California for the native people and by purchasing small plots of land for landless natives. They simultaneously began pressing the U.S. Congress to find homes for the homeless native people.[1]

The Congress eventually responded by authorizing a survey in 1905 by Charles Kelsey, a leader of the NCIA, to discover the number and land status of nonreservation natives in California. Although this survey had significant problems (tribal identification was not always accurate and the names of the women and children were rarely collected), Kelsey demonstrated what everyone knew, namely, that there were many homeless natives. He counted 520 male natives in Madera County and determined that 484, or 94 percent, of them had no land that they could use without being accused of trespass. The following year, the U.S. Congress budgeted $100,000 for land and services for native people in the northern two-thirds of California. When the small parcels of land thus purchased were turned

1. Mathes 1990: 1–18. This group was an offshoot of the Women's National Indians Association that had been formed in 1879 in Philadelphia. These wealthy women had close ties with members of Congress.

over to the native people, someone with little knowledge of Spanish called them rancherias[2] and thus was born the Rancheria Era in the history of California natives.

Congress continued to sporadically establish out-of-the-way plots of land for rancherias: by 1830, there were 36, and by 1950 there were 59. However, behind these seemingly empathetic acts there were nefarious purposes, which can be seen in the problems they caused. First, there were problems related to the size of the rancherias. It became standard practice that rancherias would be 160 acres, which to an American farmer must have seemed a generous bequeathal. For hunters and gatherers, this area was impossibly small. An area of 160 acres was just one-fourth of a square mile, but hunters and gatherers typically ranged over at least 100 square miles. This was a big problem in multiple ways. The government expected that all of the natives in the immediate area would live on the small area of the rancheria, but this meant that game animals and gathered food plants were quickly wiped out and that the natives had to go out of the rancheria area to hunt and gather on land that was usually owned by white people. Ironically, this was one of the things that the rancherias were meant to stop. In any case, this spawned a competition among the hunters and gatherers for nearby food sources. The size of the rancherias also caused competition for water and fuel among the natives.

A second type of problem was related to the composition of the rancherias. The rancherias were to be the homes of any and all natives in the area regardless of differences in tribal affiliation, language, customs, social structures, and religions. In some cases, it forced traditional enemies together.[3] The Chowchilla situation was a case in point. By the beginning of the twentieth century, the Chowchilla people had gradually become united around the Lewis and Blackhawk homesteads. Within that area, some had gained their own land through allotments and other means and others had settled in small towns nearby, primarily Coarsegold, Fine Gold, and O'Neals. The Picayune Rancheria, founded in 1908, was consequently the Chowchilla's nearest rancheria and, hence, the one that the government intended for the Chowchilla, homeless or not. However, that rancheria was also intended for the Chukchansi Yokuts, the Dalenchi Yokuts, and the Pohonichi Miwoks, and it was on the Chukchansi homeland. Political

2. In Spanish, *rancheria* means *town*, but the Americans used the word to mean a collection of native dwellings.

3. At the Table Mountain Rancheria, Yokuts and Mono Paiutes, who were traditional enemies, were forced together.

and social fractionation was inevitable because the Chukchansi considered Picayune to be *their* rancheria, because there was competition for natural resources (particularly water), and because the tribes were culturally distinct to one extent or another. There were two languages (Miwok and Yokuts) and different social customs (e.g., different rules about who can marry whom). For these kinds of reasons, the Chowchilla enthusiasm for a presence at Picayune dwindled very quickly. In the 1910 Federal Census of the Indian Population, 12 Chowchilla were listed at Picayune, but from that time until the termination of the rancheria in 1966, Federal Indian Censuses found no Chowchilla to be living on the property.[4]

Washington knew of the problems and the social disintegration that was happening, and they knew that the living conditions on the rancheria were deteriorating badly. As at many other rancherias, the roads, water sources, fuel, sanitation, and food sources at Picayune were all woefully inadequate. Still, the government moved at a snail's pace trying to make the rancheria livable. Some improvements were done, but most improvements were either started and abandoned or not begun at all. Perhaps the BIA and congressmen thought, consciously or unconsciously, that natives were people who lived in nature under the rudest conditions, so why improve the living conditions? The natives also did little to improve the land because the rancheria land was government land, not theirs. If an individual, family, or tribal component improved the rancheria, for example by developing a water source or building latrines, the improvement belonged to no one or everyone. An individual or family could live anywhere on the rancheria, but if a family left their dwelling even temporarily, another family could claim it.

Living conditions and intertribal antagonism became steadily worse on Picayune and the departure of native families steadily increased. Two years after Picayune was first available, 63 of the 120 natives who chose to be interviewed for the 1910 decadal U.S. census claimed a connection to the rancheria in their replies to the census taker. In later censuses, the number of natives who lived there or claimed a connection to the place rapidly declined. In 1933, there were 20 people on the rancheria and, in 1966, when the rancheria was terminated; there were 10 people there. This was also a statewide trend. In fact, by 1976, three years before U.S. federal

---

4. As we will see in the next chapter, the Chowchilla established an association with the rancheria later in the century.

courts began debating the fate of rancherias, a survey funded by the state[5] found that more than half of the 59 rancherias had been abandoned or were virtually abandoned.

While the struggles of the rancherias continued in the field, the understanding of native people in Washington were changing drastically as the result of the Merriam report. President Hoover reacted to the report quickly, ordering an increase in the quantity and quality of food and clothing at the boarding schools and instigating a study of the medical services for natives. However, it was President Roosevelt and John Collier, Roosevelt's BIA commissioner, who brought together a much broader package of changes a few years later. This was presented to Congress as the Indian Reorganization Act (IRA) of 1934. The basic intent of this omnibus act was to correct government policies by discarding the unilineal cultural evolution model and introducing a multicultural perspective. Government policies were no longer to be focused on total acculturation but, rather, to recognize and assist each of the tribes as a distinct society that has the right to perpetuate its own traditional culture and the right to evolve in its own way. Within this broad scope, Collier focused upon specific parts of native culture that the government policies had damaged, particularly tribal self-governance and leadership, tribal land and land allotments, education, and medical services.

The revival of traditional tribal leadership was greatly facilitated by the act. It made tribal membership equivalent to national citizenship, and the two were obtained simultaneously. If an individual was a member of a tribe, he or she was also an American citizen. These stipulations of the act made tribal membership much more functional and tribal government more revered.

Prior to 1934, the BIA exerted pressure on tribes like the Chowchilla at every opportunity to stop all communal activities because such activities fortified the tribal identity. Government agents and missionaries both wanted tribal societies to be composed of independent families with weak, if any, tribal leadership. They wanted the people in the villages to regard tribal chiefs as dictators or simply old-fashioned, and to regard the traditional methods of choosing chiefs as irrelevant and unfair. As a result, some native people who had, for internal or external reasons, lost their

---

5. *A Study of Existing Physical and Social Conditions and the Economic Potential of Selected Indian Rancherias and Reservations in California.* Hirshen and Associates, Berkeley, CA. June 1976.

leadership found themselves drifting toward small camps of disconnected families and individuals.

The Chowchilla, on the other hand, were unified by the steady leadership that would later become a central requirement of federal recognition. This was mainly because there was a solid tradition that leaders had to be members of the eagle clan, i.e., members of the family line of Jose Rey. After Jose Rey's demise in the Mariposa War, Chief Blackhawk (Poholeel) assumed the leadership as Jose Rey's brother. Blackhawk's leadership, however, took power from his inheritance, rather than from his actions as a chief. Being the leader of the Chowchilla when they were gardeners more or less confined to a one-square-mile piece of land and its gardens was very different from when they were free-roaming hunters and gatherers. Not surprisingly, little is know about his leadership. When he died in 1891, the title of chief was quietly discarded and Chowchilla leadership in a reduced form shifted back from the Blackhawk's homestead to the Lewis homestead, where Mary Blackhawk Lewis drew power from her familial connection with the Lewises and from her role as matriarch of the large family living there with her. In 1891, there were about 12 adults and about 12 children living there, and the numbers would rise quickly in the 1890s as more children were born. Then, in 1895, her husband, Thomas Lewis, died and left her the most powerful Chowchilla remaining.

Mary Blackhawk herself succumbed in 1907. She had preached the importance of being faithful to their ancestors for more than 50 years, and any one of her children could have stepped into the leadership role. On the other hand, it could have happened that none of them wanted to be the leader or were capable of serving as the tribe's leader. However, Mary Blackhawk's indoctrination did neither of these. The attention of the family focused on eight of Mary Blackhawk's children, five women and four men, who were over the age of 30 in 1907. However, the men were not considered for various reasons. Robert Cap Lewis, the oldest male, died just before Mary Blackhawk died. James Savage Lewis had found a wife among the Dalenchi Yokuts and, despite the patrilocal tradition, he moved to live with his wife's family. The twins, Thomas and Neal Lewis, were not considered, but we don't know why they weren't—possibly because they had lived away from the Lewis homestead for several years as speculated above. This left the four oldest women—Caroline, Florence, Sarah, and Jane—none of whom wanted to be the leader of the tribe but all of whom were willing to form a four-person leadership group.

Carolina (1854–1940)

Florence (1862?–1937)

Sarah (1862–1930)

Jane (1871–1951)

Figure 13. First four daughters of Mary Blackhawk

We may speculate that this form of governance lasted about 30 years, because 30 years after the death of Mary Blackhawk, the four women were 61 to 80 years old and the IRA became law. Then there was a new optimism among all natives and the four women decided that there was a person who could lead the Chowchilla by herself, namely Carmelita Topping,

Figure 14. Carmelita Romero (1902–1965)

the 32-year-old daughter of Jane Lewis and the granddaughter of Mary Blackhawk. Carmelita, whose leadership is remembered with pride by elder Chowchillas today, held the role for about 20 years. She abdicated her role as leader and supported her son, Leonard Topping, as her replacement. Although there was considerable opposition, Leonard was approved by the majority of the tribe.

Leonard's greatest achievement was, without doubt, his and his council's construction of a constitution for the tribe in 1978, which will be discussed later in the book. The constitution was indeed momentous. The organization of the tribal government was set down in writing. The leader of the tribe would be called a chairperson and he or she will be assisted by a tribal council. The chairperson and the tribal council would be elected to their seats. The rights and responsibilities of the chairperson and council were spelled out in detail. More than anything, it proclaimed that the Chowchilla was a tribe in perpetuity. Leonard was the tribal chairman for most of the second half of the twentieth century, until his health failed in the 1990s. During Leonard's last years, his nephew, Jerry Brown, the great-great-great-grandson of Jose Rey, became his constant companion, and when Leonard died in 2000, Jerry Brown became the next and current chief of the Chowchilla.

The steady maintenance of traditional Chowchilla leadership through the turbulent years of the first half of the twentieth century was a great demonstration of the strength of the culture as a whole and its resistance to acculturation. The support of the IRA, while not vital, honored and validated the tribal traditions and the unity provided by the leaders. When the act was presented to the native people for ratification, however, the Chowchillas were not given the opportunity to vote. Only those people actively associated with a rancheria could vote, and the only people remaining on the government list of natives at Picayune were Chukchansi, with some mixture of Pohonochi Miwok blood. They voted against the act.

Nevertheless, all native people, regardless of how or whether they voted, enjoyed the benefits of the act. The government attacks on tribal cultures stopped, at least temporarily, and the recognition of native peoples' right to exist as separate, legitimate, sovereign nations gradually filtered down through the American public. The natives began to take control of their own money and land. Schools for native people were made relevant and functional to their needs. Medical services became more effective and available.

On the other hand, there were many battles yet to be fought for native independence, and there were some serious flaws in the act. Political independence was hampered by federal rules and "guidance" emanating from Congress and the BIA. The rules in the act were not flexible enough to take into account the differences of local native cultures, e.g., Yokuts versus Miwok cultures. Adding the rules for the application of the act to the older BIA rules produced a quagmire of regulations that slowed BIA activity in Washington to a crawl.

The biggest flaw of the act, however, was the inadequate resolution of the allotment program. The issuance of allotments was halted and all of the allotments that had not been placed on the tax rolls were placed in a perpetual government trust. While this protected allotments from being exploited by scurrilous non-native people, it resulted in so much fragmentation of the allotments that native people could not use the land. This occurred because the allotments were subdivided among heirs at the death of the allottee and again at the deaths of heirs for generations afterward. Thus, after a few generations, many children, grandchildren, great grandchildren, nephews, and nieces would own small parts of the allotment, and these fragments of the allotment could not be used because no one knew where the boundaries of the fractions were. Consequently, no one can use their particular fragment of the allotment without getting permission from all of the other owners. One of the Chowchilla women described the situation that developed on her family's trust land:

My aunt has inherited allotment land from an aunt by marriage and my dad and aunt have inherited allotment land from their step-grandfather. There was originally 160 acres of trust land. They have never lived on this land. Fragmentation is the big problem. What has taken place is that various natives have basically squatted on this land. Most do not have proper paperwork to justify their existence on this property. Over time it becomes assumed that they have title to live there. On one occasion there was a certain individual who was going to build a house on my aunt's allotment land and I believe the BIA stepped in and stopped the development. Who ultimately is monitoring the land, I do not know. You are right when you mention that when it comes to using the land, the heirs disagree about how to use it. In the end, it seems that many people live on the land but most don't even own any of it. What a mess!

12

Rancheria Friends and Foes

After the Second World War began, a wave of xenophobia swept over the United States and the support in Congress for multiculturalism evaporated. For the native people, this meant that native societies and their leaders could no longer expect the financial support or the respect of national leaders. When Republicans swept into power in 1952, the general disinterest in native people crystallized into national policy against them. The "Get out of the Indian Business" movement was born. Under this pressure, the federal government returned to the ethnocentric unilineal thinking of the Dawes Act. The senators and representatives then adopted some fallacious beliefs, namely, that financial support was actually preventing the native people from adopting American culture; that the paltry financial support given was undermining native societies and causing more poverty; and that native societies were deprecating American culture by presenting alternative cultures. These beliefs were a revelation of the ignorance of the lawmakers rather than a description of reality, but the beliefs convinced them that reservations and rancherias should be terminated and all forms of aid to native people withdrawn. Native people had been ordained as citizens and should not be supported when other citizens are not. They should earn the same rights by accepting the responsibilities of taxes and allegiance as other citizens did.

The ethnocentric and malicious bills that were proposed by Congress were aimed particularly at California rancherias.[1] The rancheria land occupied by native people should not be given special status, free of taxation, nor should they be supported with funds that were produced by taxing

---

1. Castillo 1978:122–126.

other citizens. There was, of course, great resistance from the native people and their supporters in Congress, but their objections only delayed the elimination of rancherias. Six years later, the Republicans were able to pass the Rancheria Act (Public Law 85-671) that (1) terminated all California rancherias, (2) divided up the land and other property among the native people on existing tribal rolls, and (3) ended all educational, medical, and economical programs that the United States had introduced. Objections to this act were issued by liberal members of Congress based upon the humane treatment of people whose previous living conditions had been destroyed by the United States. But their arguments were weak compared to those of the Republicans and they were quickly overcome by the addition of stipulations in the Act that the termination plan of each rancheria had to be approved by the majority of the native people associated with that rancheria before it went into effect, and that long-delayed improvements of the land that the natives would still occupy would be completed.

However, the BIA was told by the Republican administration to tell all of the agents associated with the rancherias to present termination as a very positive goal. Their instructions were to imply that the main reason for the Rancheria Act was the improvement of the rancherias. The government had failed to improve the rancherias for decades, but the BIA agents were to promise that the problems would now be rectified, as indeed the Rancheria Act stated. Roads would be improved, water distribution systems for irrigation and domestic use would be installed, and other promised improvements completed if and when the native people voted for the termination of the government's "trust responsibilities." Most of the native people did not understand that ending trust responsibilities meant disavowing native ownership and protection of the rancheria lands, but they were vividly aware that the rancherias needed the promised improvements. As a consequence, native people on 41 rancherias, including the Picayune Rancheria, voted to have their rancherias terminated![2] As each rancheria was fraudulently pushed into termination, the BIA quickly cut the protection of the rancheria land from homesteaders and predatory white land speculators and stopped all health and education services. Subsequently, the congressional allocations of funds for the promised physical improvements were slow in coming, and, without adequate medical and educational assistance,

---

2. All of the other rancherias were thought to be abandoned. Tribes associated with these "abandoned" rancherias were left in limbo regarding federal aid and their ownership and improvement of the land.

the native people were left in worse conditions than they had been before. In all, the California tribes lost 5,000 acres of trust property.[3]

The Picayune Rancheria, the rancheria most important to the Chowchilla and the Chukchansi, was formed by Presidential Executive Order in 1912 with 80 acres, but had been whittled away and consisted of only 29 acres when it was terminated. It is significant that the U.S. government has always referred to rancherias as land rather than as a settlement or as the people at a place. The native people, however, used the latter definition. It was puzzling to them in the early years when the BIA agents told them that the rancheria had definite boundaries. It was a little less puzzling when they were told the area was to be the home of all of the natives in a particular area. There was already some mixture of the tribes on the land. The 1910 U.S. census lists 89 Chukchansi, 17 Pohonichi Miwok, 12 Chowchilla,[4] and eight Dalenchi on the land. However, when the Rancheria was polled for the Indian Reorganization Act, only a few people, mostly Chukchansi, were considered eligible to vote, and, at the time of termination, only 18 Chukchansi were on the 29 acres. All of the other native people were living on allotments and other land around, but not on the land of the rancheria.[5] If the native definition of a rancheria had been used at the time of termination, rather than the BIA definition, the BIA would have recorded a significantly different group of rancheria owners. Instead, the Picayune Rancheria land *and* its membership as a sociopolitical unit became owned by a small group of people consisting mainly of the Wyatt and Ramirez families. This set the stage for many later developments and shaped the future of many native people.

The effect of this termination and the apparent antipathy of the federal government caused the excluded native people to resume the pessimistic outlook that had existed before the IRA. The Chowchillas, in particular, readopted a low social profile through the 1960s and 1970s by steadfastly avoiding tribal affairs that might be reported in the white newspapers and by not participating in white business or politics. In the late 1960s, when speakers of the Chowchilla dialect of Yokuts were dying out, no orga-

---

3. Castillo 1978:123.

4. Early censuses require interpretation. The Chowchilla, for example, identified themselves as Mariposa Indians and Dry Creek Indians.

5. According to a letter from the Picayune Rancheria to the tribal chairman of the Chowchilla in 2004, Mary Blackhawk Lewis had an allotment in Coarsegold near the rancheria. Savage Lewis (her son and the grandson of Chief Blackhawk) and his family lived on land adjacent to the rancheria, according to BIA communications.

nized effort was made to preserve the language. When the archaeologist Moratto disinterred the bones of Chowchilla ancestors from several sites at Eastman Lake and took them away to be publicly displayed in the San Francisco State University Museum, there was no organized objection from the Chowchillas.[6]

The tribe's optimism began to return in the late 1970s when they learned that native people in the Coast Range north of San Francisco were going to court to challenge the termination of their rancherias. The first rancheria to go through this legal procedure was the Robinson Rancheria in Lake County, and, on March 22, 1977, the court surprised everyone by ruling that the termination of that rancheria was null and void. This landmark event ignited great interest among the Chowchilla, and for the rest of the year Leonard Topping and his tribal council developed a tribal constitution that was adopted on January 21, 1978, before the next rancheria was restored.

The Robinson restoration jolted many tribes into action. The Robinson court set important precedents, particularly that termination could be challenged in court and that a tribe's sovereignty is not negated by termination. However, the Chowchilla's new constitution was of little help in regaining federal support because they are not federally recognized. As far as the U.S. government was concerned, tribes were not eligible for support unless they were federally recognized with land in trust and, hence, a rancheria. In fact, an unrecognized tribe was treated as if it did not exist. Communications from such a tribe could be disregarded without response. In short, there were only two ways that the Chowchilla could regain government support: be recognized or become members of the Picayune Rancheria. It is easy to see why they supported the restoration of the Picayune Rancheria and, when that happened, why membership in that rancheria was important. Fortunately, there were always congenial relations between the Chowchilla and the Chukchansi.

After the Robinson Rancheria and four other rancherias were individually restored, a Pomo woman named Tillie Hardwick and the California Indian Legal Services began a class action case to restore 17 rancherias, including Picayune, as a group. Then, after four years of argument, the court restored all of the 17 rancherias on December 22, 1983. For the Chukchansi, the Chowchilla, and all of the other tribes who had previous or potential connections with Picayune, this seemed to be welcome relief,

6. Cf. *Madera Tribune*, April 22, 2003.

opening the door to assistance from Washington. However, many decisions about how this would happen had yet to be decided.

Five years later, Nancy Wyatt wrote a constitution for the Picayune that established a rancheria council and set down the qualifications for Rancheria membership. According to a later rancheria newsletter,[7] the constitution stated that the only people who could be members were those (1) who were on the original BIA distribution list and their descendants (i.e., the Wyatt family), or (2) who possessed or would anticipate inheriting allotment land (they already felt restricted by the area of the rancheria), or (3) who petitioned successfully for membership in the first year of the new constitution. Tribal membership and blood relationships were not mentioned as qualifications, and thus members did not have to be Chukchansi, as some had feared. Washington support would indeed flow to all affiliated tribes.

Later it was recognized that the amount of support that Washington would send would be in proportion to the number of members in the rancheria. Not surprisingly, the rancheria council quietly dropped the third method of becoming a member. Requests for membership were accepted from natives from all tribes. The membership roll rapidly escalated, with many Chowchilla individuals and families happily becoming members. However, the large enrollment caused big problems for the rancheria. The area of the rancheria, still 29 acres, was too small to facilitate and evenly distribute Washington's support. At the same time, despite the fact that the amount of government support was determined on a per-person basis, the per-person nature of the government deliveries, the absence of an efficient delivery system and the dispersion of the population caused inequality and rising dissatisfaction among the members. On top of it all was the shortage of funds to stimulate trade.

In the late 1990s, there were rumors that casinos were being built in other places and were greatly improving the wealth of tribes. However, when the native council at Picayune considered the idea, they found themselves stymied by three impediments. First, there was opposition from governmental and private groups based upon the expected concerning the economic and moral effects of gambling on both the native and nonnative people in the area. In addition, the powerful gambling interests in Nevada did not want competition for customers from rancheria casinos,

---

7. Dated February 2005. A request for a copy of the constitution was denied. Membership qualifications became a closely guarded secret in the late 1990s.

and would mount formidable legal attacks on government permission for native gambling. And the biggest impediment was California's state constitution, which made several types of casino gambling (slot machines, blackjack, and other card games) illegal. The state legislature consequently decided to measure public support for gambling on Native American land by putting a proposition on the 1998 election ballot. It passed with a plurality, but Nevada gambling interests quickly refuted it on a technicality. The legislators then rewrote the proposition and put it on the 2000 ballot as Proposition 1A. With greater publicity, 1A passed and demonstrated ample public support. This cleared the way for the legitimization of tribal casinos.

Casinos began to appear on rancherias, and the knowledge of the amazing revenues they earned swept through the rancherias population. The Picayune Rancheria was relatively remote from large cities and major highways, but, once the council learned about the level of possible gambling income, they did not hesitate to vote for a casino on their land. While their debate was going on, gambling clubs in Nevada and elsewhere were organizing to take advantage of the native people by building, furnishing, and operating casinos for them. Representatives from these gambling organizations spread out through California's rancherias, promising to do this, and, in most cases, the councils were easy to convince. The cost of the services was unbelievably high, but the profits promised were higher still. Further, the rancherias did not have to pay for the casino until the casino was up and running, and then the council had to pay them a percentage of the profits each month. If there were no profits, the council did not have to pay them. However, the contracts stressed the risks that the gambling companies were taking and demanded a very large percentage of the profits from each rancheria they served. The chairman of a tribe north of Picayune, for example, told the author that the Nevada gamblers asked for 80 percent of the profits for as long as the casino existed! At Picayune, the council was more circumspect than most and agreed to pay 30 percent of the profits to a gambling consortium from Osceola, Florida, called the Osceola Blackwood Ivory Gaming Company (OBIG).[8] In the end, the promise of 70 percent of profits, predicted to be in the tens of millions of dollars and

---

8. The financial affairs of the rancheria were held strictly secret from everyone except the council. Consequently, the information given here concerning the rancheria's casino comes from interviews of informed rancheria members by the reporters of local newspapers, particularly the *Fresno Bee*. All of the pertinent interviews can be found online.

coming with little risk to themselves, melted all native resistance and the Picayune council signed the contract.

Three years after Proposition 1A, the Picayune Rancheria had a large casino on 160 acres of land in Coarsegold, California, and money began to flow into the pockets of happy natives. However, the people were shocked when, the same year, the rancheria council began to cancel the enrollment of hundreds of their members. Letters were sent in the mail informing members that they would no longer receive any further casino money or other support from the rancheria. The amount of money flowing into the rancheria was incredibly large and steadily rising, but the disenrollment continued. In 2012, 900 of the 1,800 members who were on the roll in 2003 had been expelled, and many were Chowchilla. For the Chowchilla, this expulsion was a hard blow; they had received government support for about 10 years as rancheria members, but all government aid was revoked when the casino opened its doors. After that, they received no educational help; people who needed a bus to get to an elementary school or a high school and college students who needed government scholarships had to diminish or stop their education. After that, they had no medical care; doctors were reluctant to treat them because the cost of treatment and prescriptions had to be absorbed by the doctor. After that, they had no childcare; parents who wanted to take a part-time job to help the family could not leave the home. After that, elders who became sick or disabled had to be left unattended. It is easy to understand why rancheria membership was important to the Chowchilla and why they paid close attention to the pronouncements and actions of the council after 2003. The Picayune council could enroll or reenroll a member as well as cancel the enrollment of selected individuals.

The power to provide or cancel enrollment was a product of the concept of tribal sovereignty. In support of tribal sovereignty, U.S. courts have repeatedly upheld the right a tribe or rancheria had to define its own membership. The leaders of a tribe or rancheria were and are expected to construct a constitution in which they present their standards for enrollment, but, in practice, the tribal leaders could oust anyone they wish. Consequently, we are left to wonder why, when the Picayune council greatly increased their profits, they then immediately began kicking people out of the membership. Was it simply a matter of greed or was it a result of external events and financial planning?

In the early years of casino ownership, when the Wyatt family was guiding the council, disenrollment appears to have been a financial necessity. The elected council saw huge profits coming in but they also saw large new expenses that threatened to wipe out all of the profits. Their contract with OBIG gave the Florida company 30 percent of the profits every year as long as the casino operated and, since was the casino profits in the early years were approximately $60,000,000 per year, $18,000,000 went to them.[9] The remaining $42,000,000 was reduced by dedicated State taxes used for specific named purposes. Of these dedicated taxes, the largest was the redistribution tax which required that some of the profits of casino-owning rancherias be given to federally recognized tribes that did not have casinos. This tax was determined by the number of slot machines that a casino used. Other dedicated taxes addressed other problems, like gambling addiction, which were caused indirectly by the casinos. However, in 2003, Picayune paid only the redistribution tax which totaled $7,835,000 since Picayune operated 1,800 slot machines.[10] This reduced the profits to be distributed to the rancheria people to about 34,165,000. Now, assuming that all other expenses were small in comparison, the casino leaders might have had about $34,000,000 to spread among their membership. If so, the average amount that each of the 1,800 members in 2003 would have received was about $1,900 per month or $12 per hour for someone working 40-hours weeks.[11] This amount was about twice the minimum wage in California in 2003 but not enough to significantly change the economic stature of the average person. From these numbers, we can make two general observations about the native people associated with the Picayune casino: First, while the profits of the casino no doubt made people in Florida wealthy, the lives of the natives were little changed. And, second, in the first years of the casino's existence, the distribution of profits to the people by the casino council leaders was influenced by external forces and by good rational financial planning, not by greed.

---

9. The amount of the annual profits of the casino can be determined from the court case of OBIG Against the Picayune in 2015. OBIG wanted $21 Million, which, divided by 14 months and multiplied by 12 months, gives annual payments as per the OBIG contract of $18 million. This is 30 percent of the casino's annual profits, i.e., $60 million.
10. Data concerning tribal casino finances are from Dickerson and Cohen (2007).
11. These calculations are based upon data given by the California Legislature Analyst's Report (February 2017) and the *Fresno Bee* for March 22, 2017. The amount paid to each of the seven council members is unknown, but it was probably higher and would have reduced the estimated payments per person.

After the Wyatt family relinquished control of the council, the disenroll-ment continued, but it became increasingly more difficult to consider it as a financial necessity. Most, if not all, of the Chowchilla people had been eliminated from the casino roll by then because the earliest expulsions were based mainly upon whether the member could, theoretically, claim casino profits elsewhere. This assumed that other tribes could and should become federally recognized and would then have their own casinos. It also closely matched expulsion on the basis of not having enough Chukchansi blood. Unfortunately, as time went along, decisions started to be made on an emotional basis and some native people were expelled simply because they opposed or were thought to oppose the council's decisions, particularly their decisions about disenrollment. By 2010, the Picayune population was so radically divided by that topic that they began to be divided into pro-expulsion and anti-expulsion factions. When the council was domi-nated by pro-disenrollment members, they expelled founding members of the rancheria, i.e., members of the Wyatt and Ramirez families, and also people who were among the last ones to speak the Chukchansi dialect. The pro-disenrollment council members put up new signs proclaiming that the rancheria was "The Picayune Rancheria *of the Chukchansi Indians*," even though this was, at least in some prominent cases, rather misleading.

In 2012, the disagreement about disenrollment boiled over into physical confrontations. Two groups, one pro and one anti, competed for seats on the council in the annual elections. However, when the anti-disenrollment group won the 2012 election, the pro-disenrollment group attacked and drove them out of the rancheria offices with pepper spray and projectiles. This, of course, did not resolve the conflict. The pro-disenrollment group assumed dictatorial powers and expelled members of the anti-disen-rollment group from the rancheria. Later audits by the National Indian Gaming Commission (NIGC) showed that, while they were in control during the next two years, $49,600,000 mysteriously disappeared from casino profits.[12]

The discontent about disenrollment smoldered in the rancheria people until October 2014, when "security teams" from each side clashed violently with drawn firearms and stun guns at the casino.[13] No one was killed in the fighting, but because the pro-expulsion faction failed to submit audits of casino profits for 2012 and 2013 was attempting to solve problems with

---

12. *Fresno Bee*, October 30, 2014; July 30, 2016.
13. *Fresno Bee*, October 9, 2015.

violence, the NIGC and state officials closed the casino, citing the inability of the casino to protect both staff and customers.[14] The NIGC also levied fines on the casino of $100,000 per day until verified audits were submitted.

While the casino was closed, Tex McDonald, a leader of the pro-disen-rollment faction, was arrested on the charge of the "false imprisonment" of the security team from the anti group during the physical confrontation. The court convicted him of the charge and the judge put him in jail for a year. The ardor of the pro faction was somewhat dampened by this, but what was more important in terms of settling the grievances was the fact that everyone at the rancheria was suffering from the loss of their monthly money from the closed casino.

The casino was reopened 14 months after its closure on December 31, 2015, but the pain of the closure continued. Large fines had to be paid to the NIGC for not submitting audits of the casino, and OBIG, the company that helped the tribe obtain a casino, sued the casino for $21,000,000 as compensation for their lost income during the closure. A federal judge dismissed the case on March 16, 2017, saying simply that state courts hold jurisdiction over such cases. It was immediately taken to a state court, but the issue has not been resolved there and probably won't be because the contract with the casino did not state that the rancheria owed them money when there were no profits made.

While all of that was happening, the Chowchilla and the Chukchansi were joining forces to fight a different threat together. The North Fork Mono, a warlike Paiute tribe that historically lived on the east side of the Sierra Nevada, announced in 2004 that they had purchased land in the middle of the Chowchilla homeland (on Highway 99 in the area of the Berenda Slough) and that they were petitioning the federal government to take the land in trust so that they could build a casino there. Needless to say, this was a shock to the Chowchilla and the Chukchansi.

The Paiutes, in general, and the Monos, in particular, had never lived in the Central Valley of California, but they claimed they had in order to be in agreement with Proposition 1A's stipulation that native gambling would occur only on native land. To say that they had occupied parts of the Central Valley was akin to saying that you were a resident of Japan after visiting that country. But what is more important is that the Chukchansi and Chowchilla were very well aware of the Mono people's perspective of Yokuts and Yokuts land. To understand both historical trends and

---

14. *Fresno Bee*, December 31, 2015.

present conflicts, we have to go back in time to the beginning of the nine-teenth century when the Mono lived on the east side of the Sierra Nevada Mountains. The land there was arid and subject to drought. Consequently, they were nomads, always looking for an area with more plentiful food items. They had adopted a very warlike and bloodthirsty stance toward people that their nomadic habits caused them to confront, even when, as in this case, there were large parts of the foothills uninhabited. When they found an area they liked, they chased the occupants out, killing any that they could catch. This scenario was played out when the Monos discovered how abundant acorns were on the west side of the mountains. There they took advantage of the Yokuts' annual pilgrimage to harvest acorns in the fall. After the Yokuts had gathered the huge amounts of acorns that they needed for the year, they returned to lower elevations. When the Yokuts left, the Monos moved into the great oak forests at elevations of about 1,000 feet and, when the Yokuts returned, Mono warriors were waiting to attack. The Yokuts had come peacefully to gather acorns and they were poorly prepared for a bloody onslaught. In some areas near the Kings River, the Monos eventually became settled neighbors, but the memories of their arrival could not be erased.

One of the best descriptions of the Mono arrivals in Yokuts land was that of a 70-year-old Kechayi Yokuts woman who talked to Gayton.[15] Her story describes not only the ruthlessness of the Monos attacks, but the inevi-table revenge raids of well-prepared Yokuts. Gaylen Lee, a Mono writer, describes the highly aggressive nature of Mono attacks. They came down to kill Yokuts and withdrew without immediately occupying Yokuts' land. This reflects the Monos' tactic of constantly demonstrating dominance over neighboring people, claiming the right to take resources such as pine nuts and acorns. Lee also reveals that Mono raid into Yokuts territory were still happening in the late decades of the nineteenth century, long after they stopped fighting American invaders.[16]

With the announcement that the Monos were once again attacking them, the Chowchilla and Chukchansi immediately began working, both separately and together, to prevent the Mono from proceeding with their plan. The Chukchansi gave the Chowchilla a grant so that they could hire the present author for a few months to collect data at the immense libraries of the University of California and the National Archives in San

---

15. Gayton 1948:159–160.
16. Lee 1998:18; see also Ferol Egan's *Sand in a Whirlwind*.

Bruno, CA. The Chowchilla and Chukchansi took steps to arouse public sentiment against the casino and to enlist the support of state congress members. Gaining the disapproval of the local population was said to be an important goal, and the two tribes spent time toward achieving it in public meetings and ballot measures. The results were mixed, but more or less ignored in later deliberations. Large meetings, held in 2004 and 2005, were more effective as numerous speakers, including the author, argued against the casino. There were also visits to the offices of legislators. If the state congressmembers voted against the casino, it would make it difficult for the Governor to give the Monos the compact that they needed.

The issues were argued many times in many places, but decisions regarding approval or disapproval eluded every opportunity and the fight continued. In 2005, no one could have guessed that the status of the Mono proposal would continue to be argued in 2019! In the intervening period, the public voted 61 percent against the casino in 2016, and the Governor first approved and then disapproved of the casino. On December 11, 2018, a court ruled that the arguments presented by the Mono lawyers prevailed and, on January 7, 2019, the Supreme Court declined to hear the challenge. The only course of action that remains open to the Chowchilla seems to be demanding participation in or compensation from the Mono casino.

Epilogue

The Revitalization of the Tribe

The Chowchilla Tribe, like many other native tribes, currently exists in what might be called a cultural purgatory. When the Mariposa War ended in 1851 and survivors representing the tribe signed a treaty with the United States, a stunning cultural shock swept over them. They could not live the way they had before, but how were they to live? All of the central elements of their traditional culture were questioned for validity and utility. Remedial changes differed from place to place, driving groups of tribal members apart and threatening the existence of the tribe. Later in the nineteenth century, American representatives—soldiers, teachers, and missionaries—came to California specifically to tear native cultures apart. As we have seen, the tribe survived that attack by retreating into anonymity, calling themselves Mariposa Indians or Miwok Indians—but their culture was left in unresolved limbo. In the late nineteenth century and throughout most of the twentieth century, the tribe and all other American tribes were pummeled by governmental laws and policies that changed in one direction and then often changed in the opposite direction. This put the tribes on a seesaw, going from times when tribal cultures could be openly discussed and developed to times when it was only rational to hide and even deny these cultures. It is no surprise that the Chowchilla and other cultures remain in limbo today and must choose between gradually disappearing into American culture, on the one hand, or being revitalized into a unified, independent society that benefits the people, on the other.

Leaders of the Chowchilla, of course, knew that the first option was irrational and amounted to tribal suicide. When possible, they stepped forth and took steps toward unification and revitalization. Leonard Topping and his tribal council, as mentioned above, wrote a constitution for the tribe in 1978, describing the tribe's leadership and legal procedures. Jerry Brown, the current tribal chairman, and his council, recognized the importance of documenting their ethnohistory and initiated the writing of this book. And, recently, the arduous job of preparing an application for federal recognition has been renewed. The latter activity is particularly important because such recognition would mean considerable support from the U.S. Congress, the state, and other tribes. California tribes that have casinos, as I reminded readers earlier, are required by law to share their profits with tribes that are recognized but do not have casinos.

Federal recognition must therefore be an immediate goal, but it must also be recognized as contradicting revitalization. A closer association with Washington would clearly undermine the existence of the tribe because the adoption of some American values is virtually mandatory if the tribe wants to receive support. Most significantly, the Americans tend to believe that personal greed is always necessary in nonfamilial economic exchanges. The idea that any nonfamilial exchange could be based on concern for the common good is tacitly considered ridiculous. In contrast, a native person is much more likely to greet a stranger with food and other gifts without considering personal or tribal compensation. When Jedediah Smith arrived, intending to kill every beaver he could find, the Yokuts chose to symbolically greet him by pouring a large amount of hard-won food (grass seed) over his head.[1] However, such differences in values should not jeopardize federal recognition. Chowchilla leaders are well aware of Western capitalistic values and, with this knowledge, they can accept and even enlarge federal support without sacrificing their own traditional values. Further, federal support can alleviate current problems while providing a foundation from which revitalization can grow.

When considering revitalization, the reader should remember that the personal greed in Western capitalism has caused massive environmental disasters for the natives of California. The Spanish invasion, with its subjugation of natives and gross misuse of the land, was driven by personal greed at all levels of Spanish society. The near extinction of beavers in California and the awful consequences suffered by native tribes were, as I mentioned above, a direct result of John Jacob Astor's capitalistic greed. The unbelievable destruction in the Central Valley and Sierra foothills caused by the Gold Rush still lies in view as great scars across the land. The condition of

---

1. Phillips 1993:73.

the middle Yuba River today and many other places in the Sierra foothills leaves any sensitive person shocked, nauseous, weeping, and, most important, angry. Most recently, we are learning that power companies have spread dangerous high voltage lines across the state without taking the time and money to ensure that wild fires could not be caused by the lines breaking and falling to the ground, as they inevitably will do. Obviously, profit was more important than the environment and human safety.

Clearly, big changes must be made to stop the desecration of the land and simultaneously preserve the tribes, but, if revitalization is the answer, everyone concerned should know what revitalization means and how would it work for the Chowchilla. To answer those questions, I will use the successful revitalization of the Crow Tribe in Montana as an example.[2] Crow revitalization began in the 1850s when a young boy went on a solitary vision quest to validate his entrance into adult status and, after fasting and praying for several days, had a remarkable vision that showed the path to a new culture for his tribe. Startlingly, his vision told the Crow people to study the life of a small bird, the mountain chickadee.[3] When he returned, he told his vision to the tribe, who immediately saw it as an important message from spirit beings. As a result, the vision then became a part of the heritage of the tribe, guiding their spiritual and social life from that time on. This young boy grew up, took the name Plenty Coups, and became the chief of the Crow at a time when the traditional way of life was fading away. Before Plenty Coups, they had been living as nomadic, buffalo-hunting warriors, but the buffaloes were disappearing and they had become the enemies of two large and powerful tribes, the Sioux and the Cheyenne. Like the Chowchilla today, they had to change or die out.

What the Crow people learned from watching the chickadee will never be known conclusively, but the following facts are likely to have been observed. The Crow observers probably learned quickly that chickadees are not migratory. They live in clusters in different parts of a forested area and mate within their cluster. The second thing they probably noticed is that chickadees are monogamous; they mate for life and are frequently found flying and working with their mates. During the spring, from late April until late June, their efforts are concentrated around mating and feeding

---

2. The data concerning this revitalization was written down by Frank B. Linderman, whose work has recently been republished under the title of *Plenty Coups, Chief of the Crows*. Later, Jonathan Lear analyzed the revitalization in terms of the psychology and spiritism of the Crow people. His interesting work is in *Radical Hope* (2006).

3. The mountain chickadee also lives in the higher elevations of the Chowchilla homeland.

the nestlings, but, when they are not nursing chicks in the nest, they fly as mated pairs, hunting and building caches in tree knots and cracks. The chickadees have incredible memories. They fill thousands of these places with seeds and dead insects and memorize their locations, returning to them months later.

Chickadees are also altricial[4] and both sexes must make a great effort to constantly feed and protect their chicks until they can fly. A very large number of insects (beetles, caterpillars, etc.) is needed for the chicks. An ornithologist, Douglas Tallamy, recently determined that a mated pair of chickadees requires between 6,000 and 9,000 caterpillars to raise a single clutch of chicks. A mated pair produce 6–12 eggs incubate them for 12 days. When hatched, the chicks must be fed for 16 days before they leave the nest. Using Tallamy's numbers, this means that the parents, who take turns hunting and feeding the chicks, must find, catch, and return with between 375 and 562 insects every day, depending on the number of chicks in the nest. The parent birds take their responsibility to the chicks very seriously. If a forest fire or big storm approaches, they will guide the fledglings to safety, but if a fire or other threat occurs during the nesting period and threatens to kill the chicks, the parents will die with their offspring rather than fly to safety.

The Crow observers no doubt also noticed what happens when predators (e.g., snakes, owls, and other large birds) enter the area of the chickadees' nests. One of the chickadees will give an alarm call that identifies the predator, assesses the degree of threat, and summons all of the chickadee of the cluster to come and attack the predator. The birds have no intention of killing the predator—which would, in any case, be difficult as a result of their small size—but they mob the predator with hit-and-run pecks until they drive the intruder away.

Only with extended study would they have seen the long-term viability of the chickadees' way of life and their direct benefits for the native people. First, a prolonged study would have demonstrated that the chickadees' way of life is stable and long-lasting. In 2016, *Scientific American* published a list of birds that were facing extinction. There were 432 birds on the list, including woodpeckers and vireos, but none of the six types of chickadees north of Mexico were on the list. Despite ongoing poor and unsustainable logging methods, the chickadees are among the least affected. More significant here, the chickadees have directly protected native people and their

---

4. Chicks are completely helpless from birth to fledging.

food. Oaks are susceptible to massive invasions of moths and beetles that lay their eggs in the trees' acorns and foliage. According to Tallamy, "no other plant genus supports more species of Lepidoptera[5] than the mighty oak."[6] Thus, the chickadees serve as protectors of the acorns that native people depend upon. It can also be pointed out that the chickadees feed on bark beetles that, left uncontrolled, kill millions of conifer trees in western mountain forests every year. [7] Such dead trees are, of course, highly flammable and forest fires would be larger, more frequent, and harder to put out without the birds consuming the beetles. Thus, the birds protect the entire biome, including native settlements, from being destroyed by fires.

In summary, the chickadee way of life provided guidance for the revitalization of the Crow culture and could do the same for a Chowchilla revitalization. More than providing tribal guidance, the chickadees lead the way to a spiritual connection between individual natives and nature. From a practical point of view, of course, creating a revitalized Chowchilla culture will be difficult. There will be many road blocks and people will become discouraged by the slow progress. In addition, world-wide climate change will loom over everything.

It will, consequently, be important to fashion the revitalization in terms of being the most effective way to survive the effects of climate change while taking advantage of it to further the goals of the Chowchilla, assuming that it becomes possible to level off the amount of carbon dioxide in the atmosphere. The expected effects of climate change in the San Joaquin Valley are the following: (1) Surprisingly higher temperatures will occur, but this will be mainly in heat waves. (2) Water will come, as it does now, in the winter months but there will be dramatic differences in the amount. In some winters, the winter rain will be large enough to produce considerable damage, while other winters will produce little, resulting in droughts the following summer. (3) In the long run, the amount of winter snow will decrease each year, worsening drought conditions in the following summers. (4) Deserts, unable to provide any significant amounts of food., will be found farther and farther north in the Valley. (5) Wild fires in the mountains will become larger and more frequent. These changes are likely to scare non-natives into moving north, leaving their land to

---

5. This category of insects includes butterflies as well as moths, but moths are much more to blame for oak damage.

6. Tallamy 2007:148.

7. Bark beetles also attack trees like oaks, in the hard wood forests, but the thicker bark on the conifers protect the beetles from discovery by the birds.

those who remain. A wise move would be for the Chowchilla people to move to higher elevations. On the positive side, the price of land near the Chowchilla homeland and higher in the mountains will probably drop, making it possible for the Chowchilla to buy or exert control over land and water in higher elevations.

Revitalizations around the world are born in difficult times. Social and environmental problems both bring people together. People help each other survive and from this arises leadership with new ideas. Then, from the new ideas, comes a new spirituality and a new way of living. Finally, the tribe make their revitalization a reality by owning land and becoming guardians of the biome.

References

Baumhoff, Martin

1963   Ecological Determinants of Aboriginal California Populations. *University of California Publications in American Archeology and Ethnology* v. 49:155–236.

Bean, Lowell J., and Silvia B. Vane

1978   Cults and Their Transformations. In *The Handbook of North American Indians* (William Sturtevant, ed.) Vol. 8 (R. F. Heizer, ed.). Washington, DC: Smithsonian Institution.

Beck, Warren E., and Ynez D. Haase

1974   *Historical Atlas of California.* Norman, OK: University of Oklahoma Press.

Bidwell, John

1890   Life in California Before the Gold Discovery. *Century Magazine* 41:2, 163–183.

Bierlein, F. P., H. J. Northover, D. I. Groves, R. J. Goldfarb, and E. E. Marsh

2008   Controls on mineralization in the Sierra Foothills gold province, central California. *Australian Journal of Earth Sciences,* v. 55:61–78.

Branch, L. C.

1881   *The History of Stanislaus County.* Reproduced by the Stanislaus County Historical Society 1974.

Brownlee, Robert

1986   *An American Odyssey: The Autobiography of a 19th Century Scotsman.* P. A. Etter, ed. Fayetteville, AR: University of Arkansas Press.

Bunnell, Lafayette H.

1880   *The Discovery of the Yosemite.* Yosemite National Park: The Yosemite Association. Revised and republished. Second edition (no date), third edition (1893), fourth edition (1911). Referred pages in the fourth edition.

Castillo, Edward D.

1978   The Impact of Euro-American Exploration and Settlement. In *The Handbook of North American Indians* (William Sturtevant, ed.) Vol. 8 (R. F. Heizer, ed.). Washington, DC: Smithsonian Institution.

Collins, Carvel (ed.)

1949   *Sam Ward in the Gold Rush.* Stanford, CA: Stanford University Press.

Colmant, S. A.

2000   U.S. and Canadian Boarding Schools: A Review, Past and Present. *Native Americas Journal* 17:24–30.

Cook, Sherburne F.

1939   Smallpox in Spanish and Mexican California, 1770–1845. *Bulletin of the History of Medicine* v.7, no. 2.

1943   *The Conflict Between the California Indian and White Civilization* (4 Vol.).

1955   The Aboriginal Population of the San Joaquin Valley, California. *University of California Anthropological Records* 16:31–80.

1956   *The Epidemic of 1830–33 in California and Oregon.* Berkeley: University of California Press.

1960   Colonial Expeditions to the Interior of California: Central Valley, 1800–1820. *University of California Anthropological Records* 16:239–292.

1962   Expeditions to the Interior of California, Central Valley, 1820–1840. *University of California Anthropological Records* 20:31–80.

1976a   *The Conflict Between the California Indians and White Civilization.* Berkeley: University of California Press.

1976b   *The Population of California Indians 1769–1970.* Berkeley: University of California Press.

1978   Historical Demography. In *The Handbook of North American Indians* (William Sturtevant, ed.) Vol. 8 (R. F. Heizer, ed.). Washington, DC: Smithsonian Institution.

Cossley-Batt, Jill L.

1928   *The Last of the California Rangers.* New York: Funk and Wagnalls Co.

Crampton, C. Gregory (ed.)

1957   *The Mariposa Indian War, 1850–1851: Diaries of Robert Eccleston.* Salt Lake City: University of Utah Press.

Currie, Annie
1957   The Bidwell Rancheria. *California Historical Society Quarterly* 36(4).

Dana, Richard Henry
1840   *Two Years Before the Mast.* Boston: Harper and Brothers.

Davis, James T.
1974   Trade Routes. *Reports of the University of California Archeological Survey* v. 54: Berkeley: U. C. Press.

Davis, William H.
1967   *Seventy-five Years in California, 1838–1909* (sic.) Henry A. Small ed. San Francisco: John Howell Books.

Debo, Angie
1970   *A History of the Indians of the United States.* Norman, OK: University of Oklahoma Press.

Dillon, Richard H.
1965   *J. Ross Browne: Confidential Agent in Old California.* Norman, OK: University of Oklahoma Press.

Du Bois, Cora
1939   The 1870 Ghost Dance. *University of California Anthropological Records* v. 3.

Eccleston, Robert
1957   *The Diaries of Robert Eccleston.* Salt Lake City, UT: University of Utah Press.

Frank, Gelya, and Carole Goldberg
2010   *Defying the Odds: The Tule River Tribe's Struggle for Sovereignty in Three Centuries.* New Haven, CT: Yale University Press.

Fremont, John C.
1887   *Memoirs of My Life.* Excerpts in *The Expeditions of John Charles Fremont,* Volume 2. Mary Lee Spence and Donald Jackson, eds. 1973:34–37. Urbana, IL: University of Illinois Press.

Gayton, Anna H.
1930   The Ghost Dance of 1870 in South-Central California. *University of California Publications in American Archeology and Ethnology* v. 28:3.

1948   Yokuts and Western Mono Ethnography. *University of California Anthropological Records* v.10:1–302.

Gayton, Anna H. and Stanley S. Newman
1940   Yokuts and Western Mono Myths. *University of California Anthropological Records* v.5:1–110.

Gifford, E. W.

1922 California Kinship. *University of California Publications in Archeology and Ethnology,* v. 18:1–285. Berkeley, CA: University of California Press.

Gray, Thorne B.

1993 *The Stanislaus Indian Wars.* Modesto, CA: McHenry Museum Press.

Harris, Benjamin B.

1960 *The Gila Trail: The Texas Argonauts and the California Gold Rush.* R. H Dillon, ed. Norman, OK: University of Oklahoma Press.

Heizer, Robert F. (ed.)

1967 Ethnographic Notes on California Indian Tribes III: Ethnological Notes on Central California Indian Tribes. *Reports of the University of California Archeological Survey* V. 68:3. Berkeley, CA: University of California Archeological Research Facility.

1974a *They Were Only Diggers: A Collection of Articles from California Newspapers, 1851–1866, on Indian and White Relations.* Ramona, CA: Ballena Press.

1974b *The Destruction of California Indians.* Lincoln, NE: University of Nebraska Press.

1978 Treaties. In *The Handbook of North American Indians* (William Sturtevant, ed.) Vol. 8 (R. F. Heizer, ed.). Washington, DC: Smithsonian Institution.

Heizer, Robert, and Alan Almquist

1971 *The Other Californians: Prejudice and Discrimination under Spain, Mexico, and the United States to 1920.* Berkeley, CA: University of California Press.

Heizer, Robert F., and Albert B. Elsasser

1980 *The Natural World of the California Indians.* Berkeley, CA: University of California Press.

Higham, C. L.

2000 *Noble, Wretched and Redeemable.* Albuquerque, NM: University of New Mexico.++

Hodge, Frederick

1907 Handbook of American Indians North of Mexico. Vol. 1. *Bureau of American Ethnology Bulletin* 30.

Holliday, J. S.

1981 *The World Rushed In: The California Gold Rush Experience.* New York: Simon and Schuster

Hurtado, Albert L.

1988   *Indian Survival on the California Frontier.* New Haven, CT: Yale University Press.

2006   *John Sutter, A Life on the North American Frontier.* Norman, OK: University of Oklahoma Press.

Jackson, Robert H.

1987   Patterns of Demographic Change in the Missions of Central Alta California. *Journal of California and Great Basin Anthropology,* v.9.

Jackson, Robert H., and Edward Castillo

1995   *Indians, Franciscans, and Spanish Colonization: The Impact of the Mission System on California Indians.* Albuquerque, NM: University of New Mexico Press.

James, Steven R., and Suzanne Graziani

1975   California Indian Warfare. *Contributions of the University of California Archeology Research Facility* 23:47–109.

Kappler, Charles J.

1929   *Indian Affairs: Laws and Treaties.* Senate Document 53 v. 4. Washington: U.S. Government Printing Office.

Kehoe, B. Alice

1989   *The Ghost Dance: Ethnohistory and Revitalization, Massacre at Wounded Knee Creek.* Washington, DC: Thompson Publishing.

Kelsey, Charles E.

1971   *Census of Non-reservation California Indians, 1905-1906.* (R. F. Heizer, ed.) Berkeley, CA: Archeological Reports, University of California, Berkeley.

King, Clarence

1872   *Mountaineering in the Sierra Nevada.* Yosemite National Park: The Yosemite Association.

Kroeber, A. L.

1925   *Handbook of the Indians of California.* Berkeley, CA: The California Bookstore.

1974   Basic Report on California Indian Land Holdings. In *American Indian Ethnohistory—California and Basin-Plateau Indians,* D. A. Horr, ed., v. 4. New York: Garland Publishing.

Latta, Frank F.

1949   *Handbook of Yokuts Indians.* Bakersfield, CA: The Kern County Museum.

Laurence, Robert

1977   Indian Education. *American Indian Law Review* 5:393–413. Norman, OK: University of Oklahoma Press.

Lear, Jonathan

2006   *Radical Hope: Ethics in the Face of Cultural Devastation.* Cambridge, MA: Harvard University Press.

Lee, Gaylen D.

1998   *Walking Where We Lived.* Norman, OK: University of Oklahoma Press.

Leonard, Zenas

1934   *Narrative of the Adventures of Zenas Leopard (1839).* Lakeside Classics Series, No. 32. Edited by Milo Milton Quaife. Chicago: Lakeside Press.

Levy, Richard

1978   The Eastern Miwok. In *The Handbook of North American Indians* (William Sturtevant, ed.) Vol. 8 (R. F. Heizer, ed.). Washington, DC: Smithsonian Institution.

Lienhard, Heinrich

1941   *A Pioneer at Sutter's Fort, 1846–1850: The Adventures of Heinrich Lienhard.* Translated and edited by Margarite Eyer Wilbur. Los Angeles: The Calafia Society. Originally published 1898 as *Californien unmittelbar vor und nach der Entdeckung des Goldes.* Zurich: Fasi & Beer.

Manlove, Robert Fletcher

Suhulim's Rebellion (an unpublished ethnohistory of a Nisenan group).

Mathes, Valerie S.

1990   Nineteenth Century Women and Reform: The Women's National Indian Association. *American Indian Quarterly,* 14:1–18.

Mayfield, Thomas J.

1929   *San Joaquin Primeval: Uncle Jeff's Story, A Tale of a San Joaquin Valley Pioneer and His life with the Yokuts Indians.* Frank F. Latta, ed. Tulare CA: Tulare Times Press. Reprinted 1997 as *Adopted by Indians: A True Story.* Berkeley, CA: Heyday Books.

Merriam, C. Hart

1902   *Journal of Field Work in California,* vol. 3. Bancroft Library, University of California.

1923   Distribution of Indian Tribes in the Southern Sierra and Adjacent Parts of the San Joaquin Valley, California. *Science* 19:912–917.

1955   *Studies of California Indians by the Staff of the Dept. of Anthropology of U. C. Berkeley.* Berkeley, CA: University of California Press.

Middleton, Elisabeth
2010   A Political Ecology of Healing. *Journal of Political Ecology* 17:1–28.

Mitchell, Annie R.
1949   Major James D. Savage and the Tulereños. *California Historical Society Quarterly* V. 28.

Mooney, James
1965   *The Ghost Dance Religion and the Sioux Outbreak of 1890.* Chicago: University of Chicago Press.

Moratto, Michael
1968   A Survey of the Archeological Resources of the Buchanan Reservoir Region, Madera County, California. *SFSU Treganza Museum Papers*, vol. 4, part 1.

Phillips, George H.
1993   *Indians and Intruders in Central California, 1769–1849.* Norman, OK: University of Oklahoma Press.

1997   *Indians and Indian Agents.* Norman, OK: University of Oklahoma Press.

2004   *Bringing Them under Subjection: California's Tejon Reservation and Beyond, 1852–1864.* Lincoln, NE: University of Nebraska Press.

Plains, Lorrie A.
1991   *The Dynamics of Cultural Change: A Study of the Indians on the Central San Joaquin Valley.* Unpublished Masters Degree Thesis. California State University at Sacramento.

Powell, John Wesley
1891   *Indian Linguistic Families of America, North of Mexico.* Washington, D.C.: U.S. Government Printing Office.

Powers, Stephen
1877   The Tribes of California. *Contributions to North American Ethnology* v. 3. Washington, D.C., Government Printing Office

Rackerby, Frank E.
1964   *An Appraisal of the Archeological Resources in the Area of the Buchanan Reservoir Project of the Chowchilla River.* San Francisco: San Francisco State University.

Rawls, James J.
1984   *Indians of California: The Changing Image.* Norman, OK: University of Oklahoma Press.

Roth, George
2008   Restoration of Terminated Tribes. In *Indians in Contemporary Society Handbook of North American Indians*, v. 2. (William C. Sturtevant, ed.).

Royce, Charles C.
1897   *Bureau of American Ethnology, Eighteenth Annual Report* (pt. 2) Washington, D.C: Smithsonian Institution.

Russell, Carl Parcher
1947   *One Hundred Years in Yosemite: The Story of a Great Park and Its Friends.* Yosemite National Park: The Yosemite Association.

Sample, L. L.
1950   Trade and Trails in Aboriginal California. *Reports of the University of California Archeological Survey* 8:1–30.

Secrest, William B.
2003   *When the Great Spirit Died: The Destruction of the California Indians, 1850–1860.* Sanger, CA: Word Dancer Press.

Sides, Hampton
2006   *Blood and Thunder: The Epic Story of Kit Carson and the Opening of the West.* New York: Doubleday.

Smith, Donald A.
2008   *California and the Indian Wars: The Mariposa War.* California State Military Museum. http://www.militarymuseum.org/Mariposa1.html.

Spencer, Robert F., and Jesse D. Jennings
1965   *The Native Americans.* New York: Harper & Row.

Spier, Robert F. G.
1978   Foothill Yokuts. In *The Handbook of North American Indians* (William Sturtevant, ed.) Vol. 8 (R. F. Heizer, ed.). Washington, DC: Smithsonian Institution.

Stromberg, M. R., P. Kephart, and V. Yadon
2001   Composition, invasibility, and diversity in coastal California grasslands. *Madroño* v.48.

Sturtevant, William (ed.)
1978   *California. Handbook of North American Indians* Vol. 8 (R. F. Heizer, ed.). Washington, DC: Smithsonian Institution.

Sutter, John
1939   *The New Helvetia Diary, 1845–1848.* San Francisco: The Grabhorn Press.

Taber, Cornelia
1910   *California and Her Indian Children*. Reprinted 2015 London: Forgotten Books.

Tallamy, Douglas W.
2007   *Bringing Nature Home: How You Can Sustain Wildlife with Native Plants*. Portland, OR: Timber Press.

Traywick, Ben T.
1972   *Big Jim Savage: Blonde King of the Indians and Discoverer of Yosemite*. Published online at thetombstonenews.com.

Utley, Robert M.
1984   *The Indian Frontier of the American West 1840–1890*. Albuquerque, NM: University of New Mexico Press.

Van Dyke, Stanley
1970   *Archeological Survey of the Shaver Lake Area*. San Francisco: Society for California Archeology.

Vendor, Paul E.
1919   *The History of Fresno County*. Los Angeles: Historical Record Company.

Wallace, Anthony F. C.
1956   Revitalization Movements. *American Anthropologist* 58:264–281.

1965   *James Mooney and the Study of the Ghost Dance Religion*. Chicago: University of Chicago Press.

Wallace, William J.
1978   Northern Valley Yokuts. In In *The Handbook of North American Indians* (William Sturtevant, ed.) Vol. 8 (R. F. Heizer, ed.). Washington, DC: Smithsonian Institution.

Wishart, David J.
1979   *The Fur Trade of the American West, 1807–1840: A Geographical Synthesis*. Lincoln, NE: Univeristy of Nebraska Press.

Index

About the Author

ROBERT FLETCHER MANLOVE, PhD, began his career as a geologist with degrees from the Massachusetts Institute of Technology and the University of California in Berkeley. After serving in the Peace Corps in the Phillipines, Dr. Manlove returned to Berkeley and earned BA, MA, and PhD degrees in Anthropology. With these degrees, he taught Geology and Anthropology at City College of San Francisco and, when time permitted, did anthropological fieldwork among California Native peoples, including the Yurok, Tsi Akim Nisenan Maidu, the Chukchansi Yokuts, and the Chowchilla Yokuts. All of his work among California natives has been focused upon gathering historical information that could strengthen their tribal identities and help them revive and revitalize their historical cultures.

CPSIA information can be obtained
at www.ICGtesting.com
Printed in the USA
FSHW021006200320

9 781610 353663